Unde

Taman Tree

To Jey

Welcome To St. Croix!
With very best wishes —
all God's Blessings

Richard A. Schrader
4-10-97

Under de Taman Tree

by Richard A. Schrader, Sr.

Also by Richard A. Schrader, Sr.

HOME SWEET HOME
WALKING THROUGH KASHA AND ROSES
NOTES OF A CRUCIAN SON
ST. CROIX IN ANOTHER TIME
KALLALOO
FUNGI
MAUFE QUELBE AND T'ING

Published by Richard A. Schrader, Sr.

Library of Congress Catalog Number: 96-92000
ISBN 0-9622987-5-1

Typeset by Antilles Graphic Arts, St. Croix, U.S. Virgin Islands

DEDICATION

This book is dedicated to Richard and Moriah Andreas, my great-grandparents, who worked in sugarcane fields from sun up to sun down.
And to Lito Valls, whose work is a testimony of cultural preservation.

Cover Painting by Maria Henle

Illustrations by "Bully" Petersen

ACKNOWLEDGMENTS

As in my previous works, this book would not have been possible without the contributions of others. My deep appreciation to Hugo "Nookie" Doyles, Willie Decembre, Elvina Samuel Thomas, James Richards, Cyprian Vicars and Frank Petersen.

Sincere thanks to Hubert Hendricks, Clacia Hendrickson, Emile and Margarita Heywood, Josephine Bennerson, Olivia Andrews, Kai Lawaetz, Calvin Perkins (who died before the book was published), Alexander Petersen, Florence Andrews, Alda Forte, Luz Minerva Nazario, Noemi Osorio, Rev. Robert Wakefield and Mrs. Carol Wakefield, and Doug Nesbitt.

To Madeleine Anduze, whom I believe felt as much joy and perhaps even shared a little pain typing the manuscript as I did from writing it.

To Brenda Davis for her ever willingness to review my work and offer comments. She has been involved in all of my eight books in nine years. For this I am very grateful.

To Barbara McGregor and Eloise Burr of Antilles Graphic Arts. Barbara for putting the little trimmings on my books which make them so special. And Eloise, who knows my style and calls my attention to any errors before the book goes to press.

To my dearest Claudia, my baby, for choosing the title of this book and suggesting the cover design. I called her in New York in April 1995 and said, "Claudia, my dear, I want you to think of a name for my new book." It seems that she was expecting my call. "Daddy," she said,"Name it UNDER DE TAMARIND TREE." "Claudia," I said,"That's exactly the name of one of the stories in the book." "There," she replied. "You have it." "But, it is TAMAN TREE," I said. "Not TAMARIND." "No, no Daddy," she continued. "TAMARIND TREE." "Well," I said. "It's TAMARIND for New York folks, but TAMAN for Crucians." "Daddy," she said, "You're always asking my suggestions and when I give it to you, you don't take it." "I like UNDER DE TAMAN TREE better," I said with a smile. "Bye bye, baby, I love you."

And certainly, I want to thank my wife Claudette for cooking all those nice dishes: red peas soup, kallaloo, dumplin and saltfish, boil fish and okra fungi, other mouth-watering Crucian "ninyam," and for providing all the other wifely comforts while I sat closeted with an explosion of stories "UNDER DE TAMAN TREE."

TABLE OF CONTENTS

Acknowledgements iv

Introduction vi

The Last of St. Croix's Blacksmiths 1

If Hard Labor Was Money 11

A Woman Named Veronica 21

More About Aunt Elvina 29

Under de Taman Tree 43

Memories of St. Patrick's 63

West End Fish Market 77

Men of the Sea 91

The Death of Albert Edwards 100

How Deh Seh Wha Deh Seh 105

Paddy Don't Do It 111

Frankie Pete of West End 119

Glossary 135

INTRODUCTION

The Taman Tree (Tamarind) has been rooted in Crucian culture for generations. Like a faithful watchman it has stood its ground, parrying the blows of violent hurricanes which seek to destroy life and property. As a good friend, in time of need, the Taman Tree has stretched out its branches offering protection from sun and rain. And it has been generous with its fruits too. Who could pass up a taste of delicious Taman stew, or a refreshing cup of Taman juice on a hot, sweltering day? The Taman Tree was a blessing to parents. It gave them a special gift, a long twig that bends but not break, and stings like a bee, the Taman whip, to put on children's behind when they won't behave. No child who ever got a good taste of the Taman whip wanted more. However, notwithstanding the graciousness of the Taman Tree, the old folks say that it's quite mysterious. "Late at night 'tis deh jumbies doh goh toh have deh fun." Mysterious or not, the Taman Tree has been extremely good to the living. I say more power to old Taman. It has been a welcomed playground for the young and meeting place for the old, a place to pound melee and tell stories. Yes, stories. Once upon a Crucian time there. . . was no better place for story telling than under the Taman Tree. And now a preview of *Under de Taman Tree.*

Hugo "Nookie" Doyles is the last of St. Croix's blacksmiths. He was taught the trade when he was a boy by his father Rudolph Doyles, "Bass Dulley." And though he has been dead for many years, Bass Dulley lives again in the old blacksmith shop near the big Taman Tree on Contentment Road in Christiansted.

Willie Decembre is from St. Lucia, but has made St. Croix his home. He left the hard life behind, but brought along his story—a story of struggle and pain. "If hard labor was money," says Decembre, "I'd be a millionaire."

In A WOMAN CALLED VERONICA, Veronica Fredericks (Miss Vero), who was born the early part of this century, gives a little view of St. Patrick's School in Frederiksted between 1914 and 1916. She lives on Estate Whim and tells about Massa Smith and his aunt, "de missis," Miss Latimer, the owner of Whim.

Elvina Samuel Thomas (Aunt Elvina), whose story appeared in *Kallaloo* (1991), is back with more stories about her school days at Midland Moravian and St. Ann's at Barren Spot. Her stories are very real, so real you can feel them. Meet Father Clair, the priest, who was quick to use his hands and his feet.

Come and sit UNDER DE TAMAN TREE with James Richards of West End and hear the touching story of a young boy born in 1920. Walk with him on the rough road of his early life. Among other things, Richards sells cockle which he gets from the bayside by feeling for them in muddy water with his toes. He buys cornflour (cornmeal) with the few pennies he receives, then runs home to his mother for a meal of cockle and fungi. Richards, who also attended St. Patrick's School, has a story to tell about St. Patrick's. And what a story!

We go to St. Patrick's once more in the Forties and Fifties with Cyprian Vicars, a student of that school. "You'll hear some people say," said Vicars. "Oh, the Army, the Navy or the Marines did so and so for me. Well, I want to tell you that the military didn't do a thing for me. I got my training, my discipline from St. Patrick's School, not the other way around." The old people say "'Tis because of ungratefulness mek e gah cocobay." But Cyprian Vicars is not an ungrateful person. When he learned that a nun who taught him at St. Patrick's was still alive, he and his wife Josie got on an airplane and flew over two thousand miles to Belgium, just to say thanks to Mother Christian for helping to shape his life.

If you want to find the soul of a people, don't look for it at the perfume shops or jewelry stores, go to the market where they sell their homemade goods, farm produce and fish—fish flipping with life, fresh from the sea. Go to the fish market. West End fish market is the soul of Frederiksted and Frederiksted is the soul of St. Croix. On Saturday mornings West End fish market teems with life. And it's not just selling and buying; there is story telling too. Stories about anything under the sun. West End fish market is a meeting place where you can really see and feel St. Croix.

The fishermen of old St. Croix was a special breed. Unlike today, muscle power, not motor, took them to sea and back. The days of the row boats and those hardy men of the sea are gone, but not forgotten. They live in the hearts of their loved ones.

For over a decade, Albert Edwards has been a fixture, like the Taman Tree under which he sat at the corner of Frederiksted Post Office selling his yam, potato, okra, pumpkin, lime, lettuce, sorrell, kallaloo—whatever he grew on his land at La Grange. THE DEATH

OF ALBERT EDWARDS is about a fisherman/farmer who came to St. Croix from Antigua as a little boy to the home of his great-grandmother. He worked hard and made many friends. But few were present to pay their respect at the funeral of "Old Albert", a man who had fed the town with provisions and fish for generations.

It is said that life without music would be a mistake. But life without humor is not really life at all. A good joke and a good laugh is quieting—a balm to the soul. The stories in HOW DEH SEH WHA DEH SEH may not have been intended by the individuals to be funny. But there is enough said to touch anyone's funny bone.

When Joseph Padmore (Paddy Moore) died in February 1995, few people outside of Frederiksted realized that St. Croix lost a great performer and cultural bearer. No one could dance like Paddy Moore. He was a legend. Scenes from the life of this top Crucian masquerader are played back in, PADDY DON'T DO IT.

The stories end with FRANKIE PETE OF WEST END. Frankie Pete (Frank Petersen), a native of Frederiksted, knows his town. He can take you on a tour and tell what has happened in West End as far back as sixty years ago. Frankie Pete is a real Crucian, as Crucian as boil fish and okra fungi. He is a man with a bag of stories and a belly full of laughs.

THE LAST OF ST. CROIX'S BLACKSMITHS

He lives and works in Bassin. Nearly every day, early in the morning, he can be seen in work attire: old shoes, pants and short-sleeved shirt, and an old Army cap, and a pipe hanging from the corner of his mouth. He makes his rounds downtown in his old Chevy pick-up truck with high weather-beaten wooden railings and tarpaulin to cover the garbage he has collected from the many businesses. "Just another Crucian workman," you say. "No depth, no sparkle, nothing striking about this fellow." Not so! This man has soul. Inside, deep down inside, there is something like rich native mahogany, like fine tipet and kasha wood; there is brilliance at the core. There is something very special about this man, something we often fail to recognize, acknowledge, and, yes, celebrate. Hugo "Nookie" Doyles is a treasure, a cultural gem. He is the last of the Crucian blacksmiths.

When I first interviewed Mr. Doyles several years ago for *Kallaloo* (1991), I wanted to record something about the life of this special Crucian, something about him that might ring in the hearts of Virgin Islanders for generations to come. But Hugo "Nookie" Doyles is a man of few words. It was like trying to squeeze the juice from a sugarcane which was not ready to be harvested. The cultural and historical juices did not flow as I would have liked them to. Readers enjoyed the story, "but it was too short," said some. They wanted to hear more about this artisan, this cultural bearer, this Crucian gem.

I kept running into Mr. Doyles after *Kallaloo* was published. We would talk, laugh and joke about his pipe and about the old days. One day during one such encounter, I thought "Oh man!

Hugo "Nookie" Doyles

The sugarcane is ripe, it is time to wring, time to get the juice...to put down a few more things about this Crucian."

When Hugo "Nookie" Doyles was a boy, children didn't have any time to get into trouble. They were too busy working. They had to take care of the goats, horse, mule, or donkey. They worked the land beside their parents and performed many other chores. This applied not only to children who lived in the country but those that resided in Christiansted and Frederiksted as well. There was ample land in and around the towns where folks grew crops and raised animals. Many had to carry water early in the morning and late in the afternoon from a standpipe or well. There was not much difference between town and country life. The horse and the donkey were used by both town and country folks, the poor and the not so poor.

Some boys became apprentices to carpenters, saddlers, wheelwrights, tinsmiths, and blacksmiths. Nookie was one of these. However, unlike most of the other boys, he didn't have to leave home to learn a trade. His father Rudolph Doyles, "Bass Dulley," was a blacksmith who had blacksmith shops on Estates Betsy's Jewel and Herman Hill before the birth of his son. In later years he opened a blacksmith shop in Christiansted near Bassin Triangle on Contentment Road. It was here that Nookie entered the world of the blacksmith. When he was not in school at St. Mary's he would be in his father's blacksmith shop, handing him tools or helping the other men to hold a horse, mule, or donkey foot while the elder Doyles fitted and nailed a shoe in place. Nookie liked to operate the bellows which pushed the air into the forge turning up the flames on a piece of iron, making it red hot. His father then plucked it out with long tongs and hammered it into shape on the anvil.

Removing his pipe from the corner of his mouth for a moment to speak his joy, Nookie said, "My father could make some darn sweet music with his hammer on that anvil. Boy, le' me tell yoh, music toh mek yoh want toh dance."

Soon Nookie was making his own music on the anvil. Among his first creations were the S-hook and hoe-wedge. His accomplishments were a source of joy. But perhaps his greatest joy came at the age of fourteen when he not only made his own horseshoe but shod his own horse as well. Graduation day had arrived. His father had taught him well. As the years rolled by, Nookie began taking on greater responsibilities in the blacksmith shop. He helped shoe cartwheels, make parts for broken ploughs, and performed other tough labor associated with blacksmithing.

"I remember," said Nookie, "when the estate managers came to my father's shop to repair their phaeton and buggy wheels. Back then in the thirties and forties, owning a phaeton or a buggy was like having a Cadillac or other expensive car today. A bell was installed in both of these carts which was used the same way as a horn. When the driver of one of these carts met you on the road in your horse or donkey cart, he'd step on the bell, 'ding dong,' which meant 'clear de way, le' me pass; ah gawn; see yoh,' Sometimes the person in the horse or donkey cart vex like hell, mad toh bad. But he can't follow the man in the phaeton or buggy, it's too fast, the cart was much lighter, and the horse pulled it like a feather."

In addition to making and repairing objects made from iron, Doyles' blacksmith shop performed another service for men and women who worked in the sugarcane fields. It sharpened hoes, canebills, machetes, and other field tools. This was done on a large grinding stone operated by turning a wheel. The town folks brought in their tools during the week, while those in the country brought theirs with them on Saturdays when they came to town to shop.

Although most of the work was done at Doyles' blacksmith shop in Christiansted, other work had to be performed away

4

Hugo "Nookie" Doyles

from the shop. It was a somewhat difficult task for estate managers to line up all their horses and mules and bring them to town to be shod. In such cases Nookie and his father made the shoes in the blacksmith shop and drove to the estate where the animals were located and completed the work there. In other cases he sent Nookie off in his horse and cart to shoe a racehorse that he thought would not pose any particular risk to his son. Nookie tells of one such occasion.

One day Mr. Cyril Golden of Frederiksted, a big racehorse man, came to my father's blacksmith shop. He had a race coming up and wanted his horse shod. He didn't have his horse with him, he drove a car. And so my father instructed me to go with him to Frederiksted, determine the size of the shoes, and report back to him so that he might make the correct shoes to fit the horse. When Mr. Golden and I arrived, I checked the horse's hooves. "Bu' boy," said Mr. Golden. "Bu' how yoh ah goh doh da? How yoh gon know de right size. Yoh ain' even bring ah measuring tape wid yoh." "Yoh will see," I replied. When I got back I told my father what size I believed the shoes should be and he made them. Mr. Golden and I then took off a second time. When I had shod the horse, Mr. Golden shook his head and said, "Well, well. Dem fit! Dem fit! Boy, how yoh doh that? Tell meh? How yoh really doh that? Yoh ain' had ah rule in yoh hand and yet yoh father mek the shoes and deh fit like a glove." "Eyesight" I said. "Well, well," he said. "Ah doan know how yoh doh it. Bu' yoh doh it." When he brought me back to the shop, he said, "Bass Dulley, yoh boy know wha he ah doh. He good foh true."

Old man Doyles work was not limited to the blacksmith shop. He was well versed in the care and treatment of horses, mules, and donkeys. As a young man, before the transfer of the Virgin Islands from Denmark to the United States, he had received training as a farrier. But Bass Dulley also knew about bush medicine and often practiced it on animals. "I can tell you about the days when my father used bush and rum to treat horse colic," said Nookie. "Papa would go up in the hill through the grass and come back with stinging nettle, boiled it, added rock salt and a pint of rum, and give it to a sick horse. Soon the horse was up, eating and running.

"People came to papa for advice about their sick horse, mule, and donkey, long after he was replaced as the island farrier by an American. 'Bass Dulley,' they said, 'meh haus belly swell and e noh eat as much as ah blade ah grass foh two days. Ah try ebry t'ing and nuttin wuk. Ah been toh de new farrier from America and e seh e have foh punch hole ina de side ah meh haus foh let out gas, cause e gah colic. Dulley, yoh eba hear 'bout such ah t'ing. Noh kill e wan' foh kill meh haus. What ah mocolabe! Dulley man, yoh gah foh help meh, 'cause meh noh know how meh ah goh mek out. Croptime de right yah and ah need meh haus foh pull meh cane ah factory. Ah beg yoh...Lawd, God please come help meh out. Please come see wha wrang wid meh haus."

Hubert Hendricks, an old Crucian, who is well into his eighties, credits Rudolph Doyles with teaching him all he knows about horses. "Back then," said Hendricks, "when horses, donkeys, or mules ate sugarcane, especially in dry weather, the animal developed a blockage or a condition known as 'dry-block' in its stomach. Bass Dulley taught me how to insert my hand deep into the animal's rear end to remove the cane husk. Without this procedure it would die. He also showed me how to rub down a racehorse to remove excess muscle by shifting it around from the rear to the front in order to give the horse more power where it needs it."

Nookie liked horses and he liked to be around when his father was trading horse stories with friends who stopped by to sharpen canebills or hoes, to shoe horses or fix cartwheels. His father would begin:

One day ah deh yah ah doh meh wuk. Ah beel drive up. Out step ah man.

'Marnin,' he seh.

'Marnin,' ah seh.

'Dulley,' he seh. 'Man ah need yoh help. Ah need it bad.'

'Wha gawn wrang?' Wha can ah doh foh yoh, mister?'

'Oh God, tis me haus dem man. Meh colt dem dying like flies. Ah been toh Canegata. He seh it gah disease, ah bad disease, in meh pasture. Not ah single colt ain' born live foh de pass six months. Ah wan' yoh toh come, see foh yohself, and examine de pasture and help meh rid de place of this plague.'

And soh ah went wid he, and ah study de grass and ah study de haus dem. De grass look ahright toh meh. Bu' when ah study he haus dem again, ah notice two mares wid swelling on deh belly. Ah seh toh mehself, 'noh sah. Somet'ing wrong.' Then ah look around and ah see de mare Skylark, ah race haus.

'Aha, Mr. Man' ah seh. 'Ah find de disease.'

'Whe, whe, whe e deh?'

'See um deh,' ah seh. 'Yoh own haus Skylark is de disease.'

8

'Wha, wha, wha yoh mean toh seh?' he bawl out.

'Well, ah goin tell yoh. Da race haus yoh gah deh is kicking de hell outa de other mare dem and deh colts ah born dead. Tek Skylark out de pasture and yoh disease done.'

'T'ank yoh! T'ank yoh,' he seh. Man, he been soh glad he coulda kiss meh. Bu' meh noh ah kiss man. Buckra man wus.'

For nearly half a century, Rudolph Doyles had shod more horses, mules, and donkeys to fill a bullpen as well as made and repaired countless iron objects on the anvil. His son Hugo "Nookie" Doyles was at his side for about fifteen of those years. At the age of twenty three, after the death of his father, Nookie took over the blacksmith shop. He also became interested in horseracing and had a few racehorses of his own. "I have taken over losing horses (horses which many thought racing days were over) and win. When those fellows saw how I took a horse with a big swollen foot and in no time got him in shape and won the race, deh bawl 'Oh God! Nookie ah wuk obeah 'pon ahwe.' But it was science, horseracing science my father taught me, not obeah. Although he had gone, he was still with me. One night ah deh deh sleeping when he walked right in meh dream. 'Nookie,' he said, 'yoh doing all right. Bu' yoh need toh doh ah lil more wuk. Use de mixture ahwe talk 'bout de other week, and rub down de haus some mo'. Bring de weight forward, da whe he need de power, in he shoulder. Bu' Nookie, yoh have toh watch da jackey . . . . Watch da jackey."

The blacksmith on St. Croix took a downward climb the day the first automobile appeared on Centerline Road. But it was the age of mass production which pushed the blacksmith faster down the hill. And what is Hugo "Nookie" Doyles doing now? He is hanging in there, doing his father's work.

Hugo "Nookie" Doyles

IF HARD LABOR WAS MONEY

His short frame leans forward like a banana plant pulled by the weight of its maturing fruits. In his youth and far into manhood, he has struggled with the weight of hard labor riding him down. From the fields and hills of St. Lucia to the gold mines of Guiana, he has toiled the land. "If hard labor was money," he said, eyes full, voice breaking, "I would . . . I would be ah millionaire. Yes. Ah m-i-l-l-i-o-n-a-i-r-e. I, Willie Decembre, tell you that . . . oh yes . . . ah millionaire today!"

Decembre's days of hard labor are over, like massa days, "done gone." But not quite. It is as though someone has put stinging nettle on him, or, as some would say, "he gah fire in he house." He must be on the move. He is an action man, a busy soul, busy for his God. Most of his time is spent at St. Ann's Church on Barren Spot hill. His week runs this way: Sunday, worship time; Monday, Men's Fellowship meeting; Tuesday, prayer meeting; Wednesday, choir practice; Thursday, prayer meeting (at the home of a brother or sister or anyone requesting prayers); Friday, hospital visit; Saturday, musicians' practice. And that's not all. There is still time left to care for his plants and sheep, answer a friend's or neighbor's call to work in a garden, clearing weeds and grass with his companion of many years—the hoe.

"I'd like to talk with you about life in the old country," I said one day after choir practice.

"Oh, sure," he replied. "You must come to my place . . . . You must come. . . . There we can sit down and I will give you a little piece of my life."

Willie Decembre

Never one to put off an opportunity to talk "old time" with an old folk, before long I had pulled up in my 1985 Ford pick-up truck at Mr. Decembre's. His modest plywood home, on a corner of a dead-end road in Estate Upper Love where the sugarcane once grew tall, thick and sweet, sported a galvanized roof and wore a coat of pink.

"God bless the house."

"Thank you. Thank you . . . . Please sit down."

As I sank into the chair my eyes searched the wooden panel before me. There was an artist's depiction of the "Last Supper" on one side, and a cluster of greeting cards, more or less at the center. Then I saw a familiar face with a warm smile among the cards. It was the picture of our humble Bishop, Elliot Thomas.

"You've got the Bishop here too?"

"Oh, yes. That's him. I live alone, but I am not alone. He lives here too. He lives in my heart."

The evening news is on. Outside the dog barks up a storm. "He'll be quiet soon," Decembre comforts me. "He knows that a stranger is in the house and wants to make sure that I am all right." He turns the television off, and we begin the walk back nearly eighty years to St. Lucia, British West Indies.

I didn't know my father personally. He and my oldest brother died the same way, on the same day, when I was very little. The story of how my father and brother lost their lives began with a dispute between my father and a neighbor over a coconut tree. The neighbor who had land next to my father's said that the coconut tree was on his side of the boundary and therefore his. My father said no. The coconut tree was on his land and he had sole ownership to it.

The matter ended up in court and the court ruled in favor of my father. The neighbor, not satisfied, appealed

13

the ruling to a higher court. After many months of waiting, the court handed down its decision. It supported the lower court's ruling that the coconut tree was on my father's property and he alone, not the neighbor, was the rightful owner. Matter closed!

Following the victory over his neighbor, my father picked the coconuts. He would sell them and charcoal he had made in the town market. Early one morning he and my brother left home on foot. One carried a bag of coconuts, the other a bag of charcoal. He would use the money received to buy a week's supply of food for his family.

My father completed his business and later attended church services. Night came quickly, and he decided to spend the night in town at the home of a relative. The following day, just after sunrise, my father and brother gathered their belongings and began the six-mile walk home. On the way was a river and, as customed, they stopped for a swim.

The hours rolled by, it was already late in the afternoon. My mother became worried when my father and brother didn't return and gave the alarm. The people in the village also became concerned. Some began walking the road to town hoping to find them. One of the searchers was my father's godchild. The girl reached an old bath house near the river and decided to enter, to see if there was any evidence of their having been there. Her eyes quickly caught hold of the two crocus bags of fish and other groceries. Their hats, shirts, and pants were there next to the bags. Her eyes then covered the riverfront for any sight of them. No luck right then. But as she walked along the river's edge, she saw what she feared most. Right before her eyes were the heads of my father and brother moving to and fro. "Oh me God!" she cried. "Deh drown .... Me pehpeh and he son dead ... drown in de river."

What a disaster! My father didn't live to enjoy his family nor eat or sell any more of his coconuts.

As I grew up it was a real hurt for me to know that my father and brother had died together before I could have gotten to know and appreciate them, especially my father.

But was it true...? Was it true that my father and my brother died by drowning? As I grew older I began to question the matter. The questions began to run in my mind: How could two persons drown together like that? Something is wrong here. It just don't seem likely. Something seems strange here. And what about the neighbor, the man who claimed that the coconut tree was his because it was on his land? Did he go to town, too, the very same day my father and brother left with the bag of charcoal and the bag of coconuts for sale in the market? Did he layway them on the way back? Did he cooped up on them, lash them on their heads, knock them out cold, then roll them in the river, arranging their belongings in the bath house to make it look as though they went for a swim and drowned? Did he had help? Did he and his partner in crime lasso my father and my brother, tie their hands and feet like a goat, drag them in the water, and remove the rope after they had drown? Or did the neighbor plan the crime and had others to carry out his plan?

Questions. Questions. Questions. A barrage of questions. The questions just kept coming. But mama said, "a man life ain't he own. De Lord giveth. And de Lord taketh." As a boy I had problem with that. I couldn't understand why God could take not only my father but my brother too, take them from this world in the same way, on the same day.

"And what did your mother do after the untimely death of your father and brother?"

Well, she took up her hoe, machete, and pickaxe and went to work. She had plenty mouths to feed. It was nine of us. Day in and day out she was out there in the land, clearing, planting, and reaping food to eat and to sell in the market. She had made up her mind to work. She said that she didn't want any man to come in her house and mistreat her children. For that reason she would not remarry. Mama preferred to be alone with her children.

Mama Decembre could not do all the work alone. She sacrificed the learning of her children for food. They had to take up the hoe. Willie was one of the lucky ones who made it to the classroom for a few years. The young hands were needed to help mama make charcoal, plant potato, yam, and dasheen.

Agriculture was and is the backbone of St. Lucia's economy and Willie Decembre had his fill. However, one of his toughest jobs was that of sawing into pieces large trunks of forest trees, turning them into lumber for building. "People were building many houses and needed plenty of lumber. It took hours working with a nine- to ten-feet whipsaw to slice these big trees into pieces. That, me dear sa, was hard wuk."

Then came the years of labor in the gold mines of Guiana.

16

When I went to British Guiana in 1953, pickaxe, shovel, and wheelbarrow were the main tools. We had to dig deep and wide in the earth. While some bore into the ground with simple hand tools, others brought down giant trees with a saw. The wood were cut into various sizes and used to frame and seal the gold mines. It was like working in big long houses down below the surface. And the pay was very little: three to five dollars a day. Yes, the money was short but the hours long and hard.

When we got to Guiana, the large group of men from St. Lucia and men from other Caribbean islands, there were no houses for us. We had to build our own huts from the same forest wood and wild palms. Even our bunks were made from wood. Grass was cut, put in the sun to dry, then stuffed into mattresses made from old rice bags.

In a country such as Guiana, the men had to be careful, there was ever a snake in the grass. One day Decembre let down his guard and took a snake to bed.

I was clearing my yard when I found this thing, a snake curled up asleep under the step near my door. I quickly killed it. Still my mind was not at ease. That kind of snake was known to travel in pairs. If you saw one, you could bet that the other was not too far away. Where was the other snake? I looked and looked but it could not be found. "I must find that snake," I said to myself. "But where?" On several occasions while in bed at night, I had felt what appeared to be a little lump in the mattress but paid no attention to it. About a week before, I had removed the old grass from my mattress and replaced it with fresh ones. Could the other snake have been hidden in the pile of grass when I put it into the mattress? If so, how come I didn't see it? No, that's not possible. But again it could be. Was it so curled up in the grass that it was completely concealed from view? Well, let me see! I cut open the mattress and there it was, a live snake. Oh God! And I slept with that thing for the whole week. What if it had bitten me? The snake was little thicker than my thumb and over one foot long. And it was a poisonous snake.

After several years of contractual labor with a foreign mining company, Decembre picked up a $5.00 license from Guiana's Department of Land and Mines, and went off into the bushes for some prospecting of his own. His team of four to eight men caught a steamer at Georgetown and got off at Batica. They then boarded a government truck which took them as far as the terrain would allow. Next there was another river crossing—this time on a smaller boat. The trips were not without incident. Because of the many large rocks in certain areas, there was always the danger of the boat running aground or crashing into a rock. Like the day, the boat bumped into a large one, throwing its passengers into the water. "What a day that was," said Decembre. "See us struggling for our lives. Thank God we were near land. Even if life is very hard, one never really knows how sweet it is, until he is about to lose it," he pondered.

But the hunt for gold did not end at the shorelines. The trek through the forest came next. Decembre and his crew were like pack mules, with one to two months' supply of food, clothing, bedding, pots and pans, pick and shovel strapped to their backs. And while on the march, there was no house or hut to cool their heads. Wherever night met them, there they stopped, a hammock tied between branches of a tree — their only rest. Sometimes Father God sent His shower of blessings on them all night long.

18

When Decembre and his team arrived at the site where they would work and live for several months, if they were lucky, they might find some abandoned grass and wood huts that were used by other prospectors. If not, they would have to build their own.

During his thirteen years in Guiana, Decembre returned again and again to the mining fields to search for gold and diamonds, but there was no major success in his labors. He did find a few pieces of those minerals. However, the amount was so small that the money he received for them was barely enough to keep a roof over his head, clothes on his back, and food in his stomach. "Nothing to brag about," he said. "That's life. Some people work hard all their lives and gain little. While others work little and gain much. I remember on one trip to the mining field, about three men and I had been working very hard digging day after day for months without finding any gold or diamonds. But when another group of men arrived and started digging, in less than a week they had found a good quantity of gold. Some men would take off for the bushes and pledge never to return until they had struck it rich. A few succeeded. But others, in old age, had to be led out without that bucket of gold or diamonds they had hoped to find."

Decembre wouldn't allow that to happen to him. He found something else to do. Logging was another of his experiences in the South American country. The dense forest was his home for six-month periods. He and his team of five men flattened thick, long trees. The logs were then dragged two miles through the forest to the coast. However, there were no boats to transport the wood to the sawmill. The men had to make their own raft, and float on the river to the sawmill. "For three days and nights, we cooked, ate, sang, and slept on the raft in the sun and rain. It was tough, tough work. But I had to make a living. I had to survive. That's why I say that if hard labor was money—all the labor I have done since I was a boy—no one would have more money than I. Some people are lucky, they inherit money, land, and other property. But the good Lord knows that I have worked for every penny that I have owned. If you see me with a nail or a pin, you can be sure Decembre worked very hard for it. No one gave me anything. I work hard for what I have. God created everyone but He does not bless everyone equally. There must be some to be low and some to be high. But the majority of the high or rich people takes advantage of the low or poor people."

"Although I don't have much other than a small plywood house and the little land on which it rests, envy is not in my heart."

Decembre may be poor by some standards. But he is rich in Christ love. And that is something money cannot buy.

Willie Decembre and St. Clair Williams, fellow choir member at St. Ann's Church, Barren Spot.

A WOMAN NAMED VERONICA

I could see her now. Her head, which is covered with one of those colorful madras headties my mother used to wear, fits snugly under her old straw hat. She sits outside Aunt Elvina's (her friend's) apartment at the Walter I.M. Hodge Pavilion where she also lives. As I approach, before I could open my mouth to say "good afternoon," the tobacco in her pipe greets my nose. And as the court officer announces the appearance of the judge, she too announced my arrival. "Elvina," she sings out. "De warden ah come!"

That was 1977. The woman was Vernonica Frederiks. She was petite but very strong. I remembered Miss Vero (as she was affectionately called) as a boy in the 1940s. She was one of the women who came from the Frederiksted area on a truck to work in Fredensborg sugarcane fields. To see the men and women in work clothes, carrying hoe, machete and canebill, faces partly covered except the eyes, nose and mouth; their arms and legs wrapped as if bandaged, you would think that they were going to war. And war indeed it was! "WAR, WAR, WAR. . ."as the song goes. They not only fought tough, thick grass and sugarcane— they fought cowitch and santapee (centipedes) too.

Miss Vero's early life began at Estate Whim where she was born, in one of the long row of houses, to Adella Hackett and David Emanuel Frederiks. As a young girl she attended St. Patrick's School in Frederiksted. Back then there was no graded education system as we have today. There were what were known as Primer One, Spelling Card, and Book One to Book Seven. However, Bible History and Catholic Church Teachings were the core of the education program. And discipline was a

21

Veronica Frederiks (Miss Vero)

very important aspect of the total learning experience. Punishments included whipping by teachers as well as by the priest, kneeling for long periods in front of the class with two hands straight up in the air. And children who fought could spend a few hours in a dungeon under the steps of the classroom.

Around 1918, when Miss Vero was at St. Patrick's School, Whim was a thriving plantaltion. It produced sugar, rum, and molasses. There were several work gangs made up of men and women. But children also had a role to play in the canefield. In those days, school ended at noon and they spent the next four to five hours in the canefield. At the sound of the bell, they hurried home to get ready for work. "Noh bus, car or cart toh ride 'pon. Wen de bell ring, ah hit de road wid meh two foot. An' noh shoes, barefoot. Ten toe deh deh 'pon de ground. As ah reach home ah change meh clothes, tek meh hoe an' ah gon', sometimes 'til down by Good Hope whe' de school deh now. In dem days . . . well, de owner o' Whim was de missis, ah woman name Miss Latimer. She was de owner foh Whim, Campo Rico, Two Williams, Good Hope, an' Gaulin' Bay. An' den she pu' her nephew, Mr. Smith, toh be de manager. Well, ah born in Mr. Smith time. He was manager wen ah born."

But children did more than classroom and canefield work. They played their little games and had their little fun. There were a lot of jokes. When a new boy or girl came to school, the teacher would ask his or her name and he or she would give a funny name. One day the teacher asked a boy what was his name and the boy said, "My name is Charlie-Electric-Dynamite, Pumper-Santa Cruz Cooler, Best Guinea Pepper." A little girl once gave her name as "Matilda Williams, Bright-Bright Williams."

Miss Vero left school prematurely in Book Five "'cause de sister, ah Dane woman, had knock me in meh face an' burst meh nose. An' ah tek meh slate on which ah was writin' an' knock her back bustin' her nose. Ah was wid meh books, mekin' ah house, an' ah boy name Steve O'Reilly call de teacher, sister Asker, and seh 'see Veronica mekin' doll house wid she books.' She call meh up to de blackboard an' as ah step up she hit meh WHAP, one leather strap bustin' meh nose. After ah hit her wid de slate ah ran out o' school an' never went back."

In Miss Vero's time, the sugarcane field beckoned one and all, except for a few who took on a trade. It didn't really matter whether or not you completed school. There was no escape— into the sugarcane field you went. It was as certain as death to labor among the long, sharp, green blades of sugarcane. So when Miss Vero left St. Patrick's in 1918, she took up her hoe and went on to fight the grass in Miss Latimer's sugarcane field. While in school, she got four cents for half a day's labor as a third-class worker. After she had moved up the ladder one step to second class, she received fifteen cents a day for nine hours of work. But there were other jobs too, like picking cotton and shelling taman (tamarind) to make sling. Second class workers were mainly young people who had finished or dropped out of school and were put to do housework. Miss Vero had her share of it, until she got into trouble wid "de missis."

Ah wuk in de kitchen wid de cook. An' ah gah toh throw out bathin' water. It ain' had flush toilet an' bathroom like wha' we have today. 'Tis a big tub, bathtub. Ah had toh cart [carry] water an' scrub out de tub. Tek water from downstairs, from de tank, an' fill up Mr. Smith tub, an' bring in de missis room toh. Dis was in de greathouse whe' deh live. Yoh see, de missis (Miss Latimer) been live in de greathouse in Campo Rico, bu' wen it bu'n down she come an' live in Whim Greathouse.

An' ah had toh clean out de missis' room, clean de mahogany bedstead, cut like how de watermelon is. Ah had toh throw up de net. Now, ah was short, bu' ah gon' try. Ah can't reach from de ground [floor] toh throw up de net. Ah kneel down on de bed an' fold de net an' throw it up. An' she, de missis (Miss Latimer), come an' she buss meh one slap. She seh ah must tek meh dirty knee off her bed. An' ah tell her "Miss Latimer, ah ain' walkin' on meh knee. An' meh grandmother (ah had live wid meh grand- mother) never slap meh." An' ah slap de missis back. De cook hear an' she come an' ask meh wha' it is. An' ah seh de missis slap me an' ah slap her back. 'Cause meh grandmother never slap meh. An' she pu' meh down in de yard toh cut wood toh goh in de stove foh cookin'. Wen Mr. Smith come, de cook tell he wha' happen. An' he sen' meh down in de village toh wuk mason. Ah had toh goh wid de mason man dem. Ah had toh mix de cement. Ah had toh mix de white lime toh mek plaster. Ah bring it from whe' de chimney deh down in de village. Soh, de mason ask me, "Vero, wha' de missis doh yoh?" An' ah seh, "De missis slap meh an' ah slap her back." Now, ah didn' know dat Mr. Smith deh one side an' listenin'. Wen ah look an' ah see, he seh "Ahyoh goh home. Tek de day an' rest! All ahyoh! Tek de day an' rest."

After the incident, Miss Vero was put to do all sorts of work as a punitive measure. But the manjah and the missis couldn't faze her. She held her own among other workers much older than herself.

Ah drop top [sugarcane slips] toh plant. Ah gah a big tray on meh cata 'pon meh head. Ah gah toh wuk fas' 'cause ah supplyin' two barman. An' sometime ah even help dem out, dig meh own cane hole, and shove een de cane, plant it. Another time wen deh grindin' sugar ah gah toh cart sugar in a tub on meh head. Ah man, he shovelin' de sugar an' puttin' it in de tub. Wen it full, ah carry it in ah room an' throw it in a box. It gah six box an' ah gah toh full dem up, an' da sugar gon' stand deh, come mascavada [muscavado] deh call it.

Now wen deh stillin' rum, das another t'ing. Ah gah toh clean de strainer. An' de rum cookin', runnin' from one tank toh ah next tank. An' wen it finish, toh test it yoh geh ah kerosene pan ah dat rum an' yoh empty it in another pan wid rainwater, an' yoh stir it up. Den yoh tek out ah cupful, an' yoh throw it in ah white plate an' yoh draw ah match. An' if it blaze ah fire, blue blue, it good. Deh call it "Whim Rum." An' deh use toh sell de rum ten dollar ah demijohn toh de people livin' on de estate. De same way deh use toh sell deh sugar an' de molasses toh people who want.

Bu' leh meh tell yoh 'bout de Mr. Smith de manjah [manager] foh Whim. Well, Whim use toh had plenty yam. One day we deh deh, meh an' de other woman dem, deh in de cellar cuttin' yam bits toh plant. An' Mr. Smith come an' lock ahwe up in deh an' wen' 'bout he business foh hours up deh toh Camandan. Ahwe deh in deh, deh in deh like prisoners. Can' come out 'til he come. Yoh see, he had he rum an' other t'ing in deh. Soh he think ahwe gon' tief it an' he pu' lock 'pon e door wid ahwe in deh.

Another time he chase ahwe off e land. It was wen deh had de strike back in 1916, wen Jackson call de strike. Well, deh seh we ha' toh move off de estate. Some people went to Christiansted. Down yah people went in de Lutheran Church. Some went in Moravian Sunday School [house]. An' some went in English Church Sunday School house. An' who had family in town went toh deh family. Ah had a grandmother, meh mother mother, live in town. Soh ah went toh her an' meh mother

26

went toh her sister. We had potatah an' yam plant toh Whim, an' deh had properly bear da year, a good crop. An' bass Pete father had catch plenty sprat, some big sprat, an' he gi'e us some. Bu' one day we went back toh Whim, durin' deh strike, toh geh more potatah. An' Mr. Smith come meet us an' he chase us. "Get out! Get out! Get out! Get off my estate!" An' we ran an' went through Hannah Rest an' back toh Frederiksted. De next week deh seh de strike done. An' we went back toh wuk.

When Miss Vero was at Estate Whim, there were many sugarcane workers from Antigua, Barbados, St. Kitts, Nevis, and other British West Indian islands on contract there.

Deh come, deh gah deh wife an' deh children (da time de money went up li'l bit). De man geh $5.00 ah week. An' deh woman she geh $5.00 toh. Now wen deh come, deh can' leave Whim toh goh anywhere else toh goh look wuk. De contract is foh ah whole year toh Whim. If yoh come in August dis year, yoh can't leave 'til August next year. Bu' some ah de man dem use toh run'wey an' goh toh "Babylon" [Princesse] goh wuk. Bu' da was big big trouble, 'cause wen manjah Smith find out, he send de johndam [gendarmes] not police, whiteman wid planter hat, goh 'til up deh toh Babylon 'pon deh haus an' pu' shackle 'pon dem hand, an' bring dem down yah, down deh toh de Fort, West End Fort, toh wuk. An' wen dem ah bring dem down, dem ah ride 'pon haus. Bu' de run'wey man dem ah walk side de haus, sometime run side haus all de way toh town.

In those days, Whim, like most estates, had two graveyards.

Everybody never use toh bury in de same graveyard. Deh had ah graveyard foh who born toh Whim, an' another graveyard foh stranger. Wen yoh come toh live on de estate, deh ask yoh whe' yoh born. Yoh seh, well ah born toh Williams, ah born toh Northside, or ah born in town. Den wen yoh dead, deh bury yoh in de stranger graveyard. Dat's de way deh doh it.

Miss Vero left Whim in 1921, but lived and worked on several other sugarcane estates up until the 1950s. She also rented land at Concordia and planted her own sugarcane which she sold to the Virgin Islands Company sugar factory at Bethlehem.

As Winston Churchill loved his cigars, Miss Vero loved her tobacco pipe. It had been her constant companion for over half of a century. But sometimes the thing we love most can be our worst poison. Miss Vero, who was never sick a day in her life, except for bearing children, died on March 14, 1994, as a result of injuries caused by burns—on January 29, 1994, she fell asleep while smoking. She was 92. May she rest in peace.

MORE ABOUT AUNT ELVINA

My Aunt Elvina and I have some things in common. She was born at Calquohoun. I was born at Calquohoun. She was born in October. I was born in October. She love fungi and kallaloo, fish and fungi, crab and rice, souse, and red peas soup. I love fungi and kallaloo, fish and fungi, crab and rice, and red peas soup. She love to tell stories, and I love to hear them. Her stories appear in *Kallaloo* (1991). But they don't end there. Aunt Elvina has "101" stories, "mo' stories than John read 'bout," as the saying goes.

Come with me, let me take you back in time, to Aunt Elvina's (Elvina Samuel Thomas) school days on St. Croix, before and after the transfer of the Virgin Islands from Denmark to the United States in 1917.

I had two brothers, Richard an' David; two sisters, Veronica (Thant) an' Helena. Bu' I was the one popa an' moma use toh chook all 'bout toh live wid other people, mainly relatives. I was like a bouncin' ball, thrown here, there, an' everywhere. I was born in 1908 at Calquohoun, bu' in 1913 after the birth of my brother, David, I went with my aunt to live in St. Thomas. We call her Tan Tan, but her name was Addelade Robinson. I return to St. Croix in 1916. By then my parents, David an' Rosecella Samuel ("Bung Dabe" an' "Cous Queen") or, more personal, popa an' moma, had moved to River an' I went back to live with them. I attend Diamond School for a short time, two weeks before the first strike in 1916. Because most of the people including popa and moma had to move off de estates, I was sent to live with Cousin Lisy Morris at Castle Burke. Cousin Lisy was very

Elvina Thomas (Aunt Elvina) and husband, Emanuel Thomas (Uncle "Manny")
1930's.

brutish, everyt'ing was a tambrand whip on my tail. She never use to play.

Tan Tan said that grandmother Moriah Andreas dream her (an' I guess I use to cry too) that if moma don' take me from Cousin Lisy, I gon' die. Tan Tan went an' told moma, bu' she didn' do anyt'ing. An' so, Tan Tan went to grandfather, Richard Andreas. Grandfather came that very night in his haus an' cart (he had a haus name "Jenny"). He came first to Calquohoun. He use to call moma (his daughter) Rosecella. He said, "R-O-S-E-C-E-L-L-A! Geh een!" When he get to Castle Burke, he soun' out: "LISY MORRIS, LISY MORRIS! Sen' meh gran' chile out yah and 'e piece lodgin' wha' 'e gah." An' he took me to Fountain to live with him.

Veronica "Thant," my sister, [my mother] use to say she rather "suck salt" than gi'e away her children to anyone to live with. She also said that, bad or good, her children were hers. An' if they ever got into trouble or anyt'ing, she would band her belly an' bawl. Because nobody is going to give you their good children for your bad children.

While living at Fountain with grandfather, I attend Midland Moravian School. It was one school house, divide into two sections known as Little School and Big School. The system of instruction in Little School went from learning of the alphabet to what was called the Infant Reader. The Big School consist of children a little older than those in Little School. The levels of instruction were from Book One through Book Six, Book One being equivalent to the First Grade, Book Two the Second Grade, and so on.

Some of the names of the teachers that come to mind are James Evlyn, the head teacher, Joe James, Henry Richards, and Florence Forbes. They were good teachers bu' they were strict. If they told you once to do your work or to behave yourself, the next time it happen, they shut up and the leather strap did the talking.

In those days, if you did not go to school your parents had to pay a fine. A man by the name of Mr. Marshall of our district went around collecting the fines. I believe it was five cent a day. And If your parents didn't pay, they had a choice to go to jail for a night or two. But no one want to go to jail, so they paid the fine or see that their children went to school. Under the Danish system, we went to school from 8:00 a.m. to 12:00 noon. But there was no free time after 12:00 noon: it was work time. When the bell rang, signaling the end of the school day, the children from the Calquohoun area race 'cross Mon Bijou, leaping from cane bank to cane bank, heading home to grab little piece of fungi, carn-pork, dumplin', johnny cake, or whatever your mother left for you, you gobble it down and head for the canefield to pull grass, kill worms, or go in de grass-piece to cut grass for massa haus, mule, and cattle, for ten cent an afternoon.

We had a manjah at Calquohoun, Mr. Agard, who reduce the ten cent and paid us five cent for half a day and fifteen cent a day when we were not in school. And so a group of children, including myself, pull a strike. We told him "no," we would not work for such little money. We then learn that Massa Albert Fleming at La Reine was paying children thirty cent an afternoon or half day. And so we left Calquohoun and went to work at La Reine as porters for Massa Albert Fleming for thirty cent. When

Mr. Agard found out that all the children had left and went to La Reine, he didn't have any third-class workers on which the estate greatly depended. He then call us back and paid us thirty cent an afternoon. We had the spunks 'cause it was during D. Hamilton Jackson's time. He had return from Denmark and was a champion for the cause of the sugarcane workers.

Back to Midland Moravian School. Reverend Barttles was the minister at Midland. We call him "de honeybee manjah." He was always cutting honeycomb from which his wife, Mrs. Barttles, made honey cakes for us. Sometimes she even made buns and lemonade. And in spite of the graciousness of Mrs. Barttles, we were often a little mean spirited toward her husband. When we saw him coming in his 'beel, we would say "Fi, fo, fa, ah smell de blood of ah German man. Fi, fo, fa, ah smell de blood of ah German man...!" And of course all the children would buss out laughing.

In 1917, after the Americans bought the Virgin Islands from the Danes, Father Clair came to Midland and took all the Catholic children out of school and placed them in St. Ann's School at Barren Spot. St. Ann's was a new experience for us. We had a graded system of education, Belgian nuns as teachers, and an American priest, Father Francis Clair, as head of the school.

The food at St. Ann's School was also different. At Midland, the big girls did the cooking. But at St. Ann's we didn't had to go behin' the coalpot; an older woman did the cooking. And we didn't had to eat dumplin' and mackerel and fungi and smoke herring as in Midland School. Nearly every day we had nice hot fresh beef soup and fresh bread.

Another t'ing I like 'bout St. Ann's School was that if we got wet on our way to school we were sent home. The nuns nor Father Clair didn't want children sitting in class in wet clothes. But we welcome the rain. Even when it was not raining too heavily, some children made sure they found a pool of water somewhere in the road to lay in. However, being sent home 'cause we were soaking wet didn't mean that we went straight home. There was other t'ings to do like picking coconuts and feasting on coconut jelly and coconut water. Mrs. Barttles, God bless her soul, was a kind lady and fine seamstress who had extra clothing on hand for boys and girls for rainy days. Once at Midland there was no letting out before school end, even if it pour.

But, like Midland, we had to be on time for school and do our work in class. Otherwise it was licks in your tail. The nuns were nice but strict. Some children live as far away as La Vallee but it didn't matter. Everyone had to be to school on time. School began at 8:00 a.m. The church bell rang three times in the mornings to alert children who were still on their way. It rang around 7:15 a.m., 7:30 a.m., and 8:00 a.m. If you were late ten minutes, you got ten lashes, five in each hand. But if you were late fifteen minutes or more, you had to kneel and receive your punishment on your bottom foot.

And don't let them have to send for your parents because of rude behavior in school. That was serious trouble. One day a boy name Rudolph Samuel was rude to his teacher, and the teacher, a nun, unknown to him sent word home to Rudolph's mother about his behavior. His mother came to school the following day. She was a tall strapping woman and she had a bullskin whip over her shoulder like a man. She made him stand on the platform facing all the children. "Rudolph," she said, "yoh beg Mother pardon right now." And he did. "Now, she said, "kneel down deh!" And she hand him couple bullskin whip 'cross his back.

Nevertheless, with all that strictness, we sometimes manage to fire a few licks at the nuns. And they couldn't fire back, because they didn't know what we were saying. We were "slangin' them" but they didn't know it.

"Mudda, ah da ah bou.
Ah gah santapee foh bite yoh.
Mudda, ah who ah sew foh you?
Tipet in meh leba hole, doan bother meh.
Ah da foh lick you."

When we weren't throwing words at "mudda," we were making jokes about one another or someone else. During the hurricane of 1916, the people of Barren Spot sought shelter in St. Ann's Church. They brought with them some personal belongings. One Bajan man brought a cornflour bag he probably used for his lodgin' and hang it over a statue of the boy Jesus and it fell, breaking the arms. The children made a joke of it. They said, "De Bajan man cornflour bag bruck down li'l Jesus hand," and what a laughing that was.

Who was Father Francis Clair? Father Clair was a no-nonsense priest who like to use his hands and feet. He will hit you. But no one else better not laid their hands on you, he'll fight them for you.

Barren Spot village was right outside St. Ann's Church yard. There were two long rows of house to the north, another row of house to the south, and a group of houses to the east. One day a girl complained that a man in one of the houses had made a nasty remark to her. Father Clair left what he was doing and went after the man whom he met cooking. After some exchange of words, he haul off and kick the man's pot off the fire.

On another occasion, one of the big boys in school went to Confession and told Father Clair what he had done. When he was through, Father told him to wait outside for him. When he came out, he hit the boy one kick, nearly knocking him over the Communion rail. "Don't you ever do that again," he said. "You wait until you 'come a man!"

Then there was Matilda—we call her "Mattie." I don' know wha' she did to deserve such punishment. . . . One day Father Clair hit her one cuff, knocking her upside down. After that, poor Mattie didn't return to school.

Father Clair taught the boys music. But one boy, Reggie, didn't do too well at all, no matter how much Father explain the lessons. One day, after trying for some time without success to explain the lesson to Reggie, Father Clair ups and drove Reggie one kick. Following the incident, Reggie's father remove him from St. Ann's and placed him in Diamond School. He did very well there and learned to play the saxophone. Many years later in New York, he played professional music. But his old schoolmates never forgot the incident. "T'ank God for Father Clair," they told him, "because if it were not for him, you never would have learn to play music."

One day we were having Confirmation lessons in the church. When Father Clair finish the instructions, he came out and began looking for Jimmy, his driver, but Jimmy was nowhere in sight. I don't know who put him up to it. . . . Father's search took him to Bonne Esperance [about three miles from Barren Spot]. As he came through a cane range, he found Jimmy talking to Ena, one of the big girls at school. Father Clair didn't ask any questions, but he buss Ena one slap. The next school day was a Monday. We had Mass before class. After the service, in front of all the children, he suspended Ena from school and mention the reason why. And as for Jimmy, he fired him too.

[In 1916, Father Clair went to the different estates calling on Catholics, soliciting money to help repair St. Ann's Church which was damaged by the hurricane. When he visited the home of Louisa Richards (later Louisa Farrelly), he found her in her yard cooking with pot on the t'ree foot, and requested a small donation. "Father," replied Miss Louisa, "meh noh ha' noh money toh gi'e yoh tedey. And further more, meh is ah woman who doh t'row money ina church ebry Sunday." "But you must have a little money to spare," he persist. "Father," said Miss Louisa. "Yoh noh hear wha' meh ah tell yoh? Ah ain' gah an' dat's dat!" A little before Father Clair arrived, Miss Louisa had finished cutting pieces of wood and her tammyhawk bill (sugar cane bill) was on the ground nearby. While she held her head down, tending the fire, she noticed that Father Clair was lifting his long black cassock and moving his feet. "Father," she said, "ah wha' yoh ah doh? Ah hear 'bout yoh. Bu' if only hoist yoh foot ah chop um clean off. Be (by) Jesus Christ, ah chop um off." "You are a devil," he said, "and you will burn in hell." "Yeah," she said. "De two ahwe. God blast yoh. . . ."]

One day a group of children from Peter's Rest were on their way to school. Among them were Velda Newton,

Marie Schuster, an' Ezekiel Brooks. A man name Hansen was approaching them in his car. When they saw him coming, several of them got in the path of the car, walking in a way as if to dare the driver to hit them (you know how kids are sometimes). "Ah who da buckra be ah drive da' 'beel? Ah dare 'e foh hit ahwe." The man stop he car and they all ran, except Velda. She knew she had not done anything wrong and continue walking. Hansen got out of his car, grabbed Velda, and put a squeezing on her. It affected her so much that she got sick. Father Clair didn' wait for Velda parents to take action. He took the matter in his hand and took the man to court. I am not sure of the disposition of the case, whether Hansen was jailed or he had to pay a fine.

Another girl, Veronica, was not in school foh several days. On the third day, Father Clair became very concern, jump in his car and took off for the Mary's Fancy area where she lived to find out what happen to her. The road to her house was quite rough. The car could only go to a certain point, almost a mile from Veronica's house. So Father Clair got out and continued on foot. When he reached, he found Veronica with a high fever and very sick. He did not tarry. He put her on his back and was away down the road to his car and to the hospital (the Steeple Building in Christiansted). But it was too late. When he got there, Veronica was dead. Her parents thought she had kanal which cause the fever. But it turn out to be a severe case of appendicitis.

In 1918 few boys had a haus or donkey of their own. Wherever they went they were carried by their own two feet. They often had to go from one estate to another to work or run errands for their parents. Additionally, children had to walk long distances to school. They came from as far as La Vallee to St. Ann's. One means of getting from one place to another more quickly was by the use of wheels. Not cars, not bicycles, not even haus and donkey carts, just by a plain, simple old wheel. There were two types of wheels, the oval and the bull tongue. The first was smaller than the second. The boys pushed those wheels with what we called "hoosha." The harder they pushed the wheel, the faster they had to run to keep up with it. The boys raced one another to and from school on the public roads. A few years before, this might not have been dangerous since there was only a handful of cars and trucks on the island. But as the years progress, the number of automotive vehicles increase. Nearly every boy at St. Ann's had a hoosha-wheel. Father Clair was ever mindful of the safety of the children of St. Ann's. One morning when the boys came to school with their hoosha-wheels, he took them away and threw them in an old dump near the mill. The boys were hot as fire. But little they could do. And complaining to their father or mother was of no use. The wheels were gone and gone for good.

Father Clair was as outspoken as he was aggressive. During his Sunday morning sermons, he lash out against common-law marriage, saying that it was a sin, a big sin, and urged those in such relationships to get right with God, because God didn't like it. But he did more than talk in church about it. He went from estate to estate, confronting those Catholics living under common law, telling them point blank to their faces that they were living in sin, challenging them to do something about it. As a result, many got married.

In the absence of Father Clair, Father Agard took over. One Sunday during his sermon, he lamented the state of the children's toilets. "They are terrible," he said. "Terrible! Terrible! You go in the boys' toilet and they have this 'F' word written all over the place. You go in the girls' toilet and they have it too. This f...ing got to stop!" Everybody was shocked. You should have seen those old people faces. Their expressions said it all. "Yoh mean foh tell me, Father ah talk dem talk soh ina church? Oh Lawd, foh he tongue noh gah noh Sunday 'tal." Moma was there with us. When the service was over, as soon as we were out of the church yard, she said, "Watch yah! If ahyoh only tell ahyoh pa-pa wha' father seh...." You see, they were always at ends about religion. Popa was Moravian, not Catholic.

Every year at the end of school, we had exhibition of all our work. Parents were invited to come and see what their children had done. Moma was always there. But one year I was so embarrass. You see, I always had a problem with my i's and t's. During the exhibition my copybook was there with the essays I had written. And on one page in the copybook was a note from Mother Leona, written in large letters. "PLEASE, ELVINA, REMEMBER TO DOT YOUR I'S AND CROSS YOUR T'S."

Bible History was my best subject, Music my worst. While I always got a 100 in Bible History, in Music I got 50. Ann Stanley and I were in the same boat when it came to music. Like me she couldn't sing a lick. Mother Leona use to say we were singing one degree above talking. When I told my friend, Miss Gathie "Lime Juice," the joke she said, "Bu' Elvina, wha' yoh t'ink 'bout me? Me caan' sing neither. If me sing, ah mek child tek medicine."

Those were the days of Aunt Elvina, at Midland Moravian School and St. Ann's School at Barren Spot, days long gone, but warmly remembered.

Aunt Elvina (Elvina Thomas) climbs coconut tree in Virgin Gorda, W.I. at age 70.

James Richards

UNDER DE TAMAN TREE

When James Richards was a little boy in the 20s, he often went to the fish market—Frederiksted Fish Market—to bathe in the sea. Today, seventy years later, he goes to "fish market" not just to bathe anymore (although he occasionally takes a dip) but to catch fish, clean fish, and talk. Yes, talk, under de Taman tree. And what does the old "West Ender" talk about? Three guesses, please...only three. You said sports? Politics? Religion? Well, not quite. But you may get the picture by using only two words.... Let's try again.... Did you say talk "old-time"? Bravo! You've got it right. Oh yes! Talk about old-time St. Croix, particularly West End.

Like the friendly old watchman, who faithfully makes his rounds in all kinds of weather, Richards is always there under de Taman tree, nearly six days a week, cleaning fish and talking with friends, men and women. Sometimes his sister Clacia Hendrickson comes for her fish and to throw a word or two.

I have tried to capture Richards' conversations—no—experiences on several occasions. And now without further ado, I present to you James Richards, in his own words, under de Taman tree.

I was born in Williams, near Sprat Hall, on September 17, 1920. But on September 17, 1989, the day of Hurricane Hugo, I had no birthday celebration. I was right deh in meh house. I had a rope and tie it to de door to prevent de wind from openin' it. But when de calm came I untie de rope and took a walk by Nesbitt Clinic. I said to mehself, those people ain' know wha' deh talking 'bout. De hurricane done gone. But when I got back, dat's when hell start. . . . I didn't tek off meh clothes during de earlier part of de night, I was deh in meh bed listening to meh radio and watchin' guard. But when I return, I tek off meh clothes and went to bed. Then I hear this t'ing coming 'cross deh, WOOOO WOOOO WOOO. . . . It sound like a ra ra. Then it got stronger. . . . Then it fade away. It came back again, stronger and stronger, a real stronger wind. An' pieces of galvanize start landin' on de roof of de house. So I got up and tighten de rope. I fall asleep and in de morning I went outside. An' what a mash-up!

When I was 'bout six years old, I travel to St. Thomas quite often with meh grandmother on a sailing boat. I return in 1926 and went to St. Patrick School. But before I get to St. Patrick School, which is a story in itself, leh meh tell you 'bout somet'ing else.

First we were living on a hill at Sprat Hall in de old village. Then we, meh mother and I, moved to Foster, not too far from de fish market. Deh was a carousel in de area west of de present Frederiksted Post Office, where Sam Davis lives, near de gas station. Meh mother send meh to get some fraico. She give meh a sa'mon can to put it in. . .five cent fraico. I, like a fool, bought de fraico as soon as I got deh and when de carousel start to roll, I stood deh watching de ferris wheel and de merry-go-round, and when de ice melt, I drink down de fraico. I wanted to mek sure I tek home de can full. But when I got home de can was full of sweet water. And meh mother beat meh. She was pregnant and wanted nothing more than a nice can of fraico.

There was an old man in Foster by de name of Jimbo. He heard meh screamin'—we lived in de last long row of house. Meh father happen to come up in de village dat night (he wasn' livin' with meh mother). And so Jimbo told meh father he should go and see wha' de problem was 'cause it looked like meh mother was trying to kill meh. Dat same night he took meh to live wid him. From then I was back and forth wid him all about. And he was one of those men who had 'bout two or three women. So when he fell out wid one, I was wid him wherever he went. I had a li'l bag and meh li'l two piece of clothes was always packed. So whenever he seh "come let's go," I followed him. He carried meh to another woman. I stayed deh a few days. Then when he and de woman got back together, I moved again wid him.

After de hurricane in 1928, we live out at Richardson Northside, out deh where Brow dem use to own. From deh I walked to St. Patrick's School every day. De nun dem were good. But one of them put meh out of school. I am not a violent person, but if you bothers meh or you hit meh, I gon' fight.

There was a fellow. . . he is still alive. His name is Alvin Milligan, Granville Milligan brother. In school de desks were arranged in a row. De back of one desk was de backrest for de person sitting in de desk in front of you. Alvin Milligan was de guy sittin' in front of meh. We had just gone in de fifth grade. De teacher, Mother Diphna, had warn us that we were getting to be big children and she didn't want any more paper and pencils on de floor. De desk had a li'l groove in it for a pencil. There was also a built-in slot for an ink pot.

So he, Alvin, wid his laziness, droop down in his desk wid his feet all de way forward under de desk. When he try to get up to stretch, he tilt de front of meh desk. Meh pencil rolled over and drop on de floor and I reach down to pick it up. Remembering what Mother Diphna had said, I tried to bend down and snatch it up quickly, but Alvin stamp his foot on meh hand. I pull meh hand from under his foot and meh fingers got scraped on de concrete floor. I tek up meh ruler and I whack him in his head, breaking de ruler in three. He was taller than me, bu' we might have been de same age. I was sitting down in de desk when he fly on meh and I just grab him in his chest and by he waist and I got him up a bit off his feet. We then rolled out de desk to de floor.

Mother Diphna was at de blackboard writing short or long division. When she heard de commotion, she drop she book and took up a leather strap. Out de corner of meh eye, I could see her unrolling de strap and walking fast toward us. When she reached, I swung under Alvin and held him up to tek de blows. She ain' hit him. But she grab meh by meh ear and pull meh up on meh feet and carried meh in front of de blackboard and mek meh kneel down. Now all this time de class is in an uproar and James Bennerson ("Big B"), Alexander Farrelly (former governor), Joe Milligan, and de other children jump up on de desk and carryin' on like when yoh deh in cockfight.

Now, I deh on meh knees. "Kneel there," she seh, "until I am finished writing. When I am through, I'll take care of you." When she finished writing on de blackboard, she told meh meh punishment goin' to be ten lashes. I ain seh nuttin', 'cause I had noh choice. But she goin' beat meh and didn't even inquire wha' we were fightin' 'bout. Da wha' bu'n me.

De punishment was suppose to be ten lashes in meh hand. And if she miss she would start over. When she start to beat meh, I pull back meh hands couple time. Then she seh, any time she miss after this de punishment would be increase by ten. When it reach to fifty I told her, "meh ain' teking no more punishment." Then she seh to meh, "When you decide to take your punishment let me know. Because you are not going back to your desk until you do."

When time came for recess I went out. When recess was over, I had to go back on meh knees near de blackboard. De blackboard had three li'l steps. So I kneel down and rest half of meh behind on de edge of one of de steps. And she come and she pull meh off. "I said to kneel, not sit!" An' so I straighten up and kneel down properly. De next day she bring Mother Superior. I am still on meh knees in front de blackboard. Deh deh in deh Flemish goin' on and t'ing. Maire Richards, de nurse, cut een. Mother Superior, she gah a piece of bridle rein in she hand. I watchin' dem out de corner ah meh eye. She too ain' ask nobody any question. She ain' seh a word to Alvin, she ain' ask meh, but she coming after meh with her leather strap. Mother Superior is standing near meh now, with leather strap in hand, ready to strike. I didn't use to wear shoes and I know what she was goin' do. She gon step on meh pant's foot and beat meh on meh bottom foot. I jump up. I seh yoh..."yoh ain' gon beat meh on meh bottom foot! Not yoh! Yoh won't kill meh." (I remember de old people dem use to seh dat's how deh use to kill coolie. Deh seh if yoh beat a coolie on he bottom foot, he die. It was somet'ing 'bout deh blood pressure was very high and when yoh beat dem on deh bottom foot, it affect dem.) "Well," she seh, "you can't come to school until you take your punishment."

I was wid meh mother again. We was livin' at Concordia. Although deh told meh not to come back to school 'til I was ready to tek meh punishment, I left home every marnin' foh school. But I just pass by de school and went straight to fish market to bathe in de sea. In dem days Concordia gut was full of water. So in de afternoon I stop by de gut. I mek soh. . .and wash 'round meh ears that meh mother won' see de salt. De water salt has a way of dryin' up on yoh. I didn't wan' to leave any evidence foh meh mother toh find.

De problem had started on a Monday, and on de Friday Mother Diphna send a note to meh mother wid a girl name Magret Frazer. Meh mother ask me where do I go when I leave home in de marnin' foh school, and I seh, school. She seh, "well Mother Diphna seh yoh ain' deh in school." I then tol' her de truth. Bu' she didn't beat meh.

De following Monday meh and meh mother went to school. De Father Superior, Mother Superior, Mother Diphna, and Maire Richards, de Red Cross nurse, were there. (Maire Richards use to come and tek us to de dentist and soh on.) All dis time I deh in de classroom, kneeling down like I sehing meh prayers. Deh been deh foh a while. When deh get through, meh mother come by de door and seh, "come boy. Leh ahwe goh." I figured she was gon' carry meh to Dane School, de old High School, but we went home instead. So, from then I stop school. That was in 1932.

De Depression was on. There was a fellow name Frank Francis, deh call he "Wonderful Conch." He also live in Concordia wid he mother. He carry meh up to Gauling Bay, up deh in Carlton, above Good Hope, and show meh whe' to goh to dig cockle. I use toh goh dig cockle and come here to de vegetable market and sell cockle, five foh a cent. I use to hustle. As soon as I mek enough, I buy cornmeal, goh home, and meh and meh mother eat fungi and cockle.

Let meh tell yoh 'bout somet'ing that happen to meh while I was livin' in Concordia which cause Judge D. Hamilton Jackson to rough meh up.

There was a man by de name of Chase who lived in Diamond. He had a daughter whose name was Elaine. On Fridays Elaine and other children from Diamond School would come to West End to play basketball and volleyball wid de children at Dane School. I had a friend name Joseph, Frank Francis brother (he died while in de Navy). Joseph and I use to goh to Hogensborg gut. He goin' goh look hog meat [hog feed]. I goin' goh cut grass. Dis day we goin' up de road in a donkey-cart and we meet dem girls by Carlton bridge. Joseph stop de donkey-cart, got out, and start to bother one of de girls. She was Elaine, Chase daughter. She was very big for her age, fully developed. When Joseph bother de gel, she grab he and shake he like soh.... And when she loose he, he drop down. He been deh on de ground a li'l while. So when I goh to him, I seh, "Joe, Joe...man come. Leh ahwe goh, leave de gel alone." Wid that, she grab meh. And when she grab meh, I jump back...I bob and weave a li'l bit and I hit her and she fall down. De gel went home and complain meh to her mother and father. De father left Diamond and went to de court in West End to tek out a summons against meh. On he way back, he came to Concordia and tell meh mother I had toh goh to court. When I went to court, I meet Judge Jackson. It come like he had x-ray eyes to see through yoh. He use to stare at yoh soh.

"How old are you?" he seh.

"Thirteen," I seh.

"Speak up!" he seh.

"T-h-i-r-t-e-e-n," I seh.

"Look at you. Vagabond! Good-for-nothing! You're not even out your shell and you know how to beat up a woman!"

He seh to Chief Smith, "Come! Take him down and give him fifteen lashes!"

Chief Smith put his hand on meh shoulder and walk meh to de back door of de courthouse. He seh, "come buddy. Go down the stairs and wait for me." When I geh to de bottom of de stairs, I look up but meh ain' see Chief Smith comin'. I had a bicycle down deh. So I seh to mehself, I gon mek a dash foh it on meh bicycle. Because if he tell meh to goh down deh and I was such a fool to goh down deh and wait foh licks . . . then, he should kill meh foh bein' dat stupid. So I lift de bicycle by de front wheel, went through de gate, and head up Lagoon Street. I went 'round de gut, burst out by La Grange, and head foh Concordia. And foh a week I ain' went toh town. Well, I get away from dat licking. In dem days 'tis a man deh call "Bruk Iron" use to hold yoh down foh dem to beat yoh. I can't remember he right name, bu' he was Joe Nanton's brother. He been in jail and he was a strong man, real ruffian. "Mun" Jackson, de prison driver, had 'fraid he. Yes, da "Bruk Iron" use to hold down de boys dem when deh come to de Fort to geh licks. But I believe Chief Smith gi'e meh a break, because he feel I wasn't guilty of wha' happen.

I also live in Upper Mount Pleasant wid meh mother. From deh we move to St. George and dat's when I start to work wid Mr. Griffith in Bag [Bog of Allen]. How I get toh work wid him? It had a man deh call Hubert Burke. He had a daughter call Clemmy. Her father is who carried meh to Bag to Mr. Griffith to help pick mango and t'ing. He had own Bag. Bag went from Mount Pleasant line to somewhere up on a hill by Grove, come back down along St. George line. Yoh goh west to Beck Grove line and yoh goh back across either Mont Pellier or Two Friend. After I goh up deh to pick mango and t'ing...I think it was planting season, planting tania. I think de tania season was from May to October. Deh gi'e meh de job to cut de tania bits. I also had to supply planters like Gustave Richards, Lenard "Chooksen" Schrader, Leroy Williams, and "Feni" Lang. And soh, I would deh deh behin' a pile of tania bits, high like a refrigerator and spread off. And I suppose toh cut dem and drop dem behind dem man who plant dem. I had to keep dem busy, da mean I had to wuk real hard. And Mr. Griffith would be deh under an orange tree, and he deh under da tree from marnin' just watchin', seein' us work. Five minute to eight, he blow de whistle toh set us een. Five minute to twelve, he blow de whistle foh lunch. Five minute to one, he blow again foh us to return to work. Five minute to four, he blow de whistle...da was quitting time.

When I first went deh toh work, he gi'e meh two bucket toh carry de tania bits. And wha' I use to do: After de first day I work, I get a crocus bag and I tie a rope on each end.... I cut it open like a hammock and tie it 'cross here. . . . I gah one on each side of meh. So when I tek a load, like seh from da corner to yah, it use to be a lengt' of land 'bout 150 feet. I had notice when I was usin' a bucket to carry de tania bits, when I walk a couple steps de bucket empty. Each time I had toh goh and come back before I finish a row. Bu' after I start usin' de crocus bag, I could drop three rows one time. This way I would be ahead of dem fellows doing de plantin' all de time.

I was meking twenty cents a day because I was workin' second class. De older fellows were meking forty cents a day. Deh was working first class.

When Saturday come, Mrs. Griffith use to goh 'round in a haus and cart selling. She use to bring a li'l bit of de tania dem. . . like de ends of de tania dem wha' bruk off. . . de ends of de small ones. . . and de potato and sometimes eggplant and t'ing and gi'e meh mother.

Now wid da dollar I mek foh de week, I gi'e meh mother and she would goh to town to shop. It was Depression time. She tek de bus from St. George to West End and pay five cents either way. Wha' people use to buy then was cornmeal, white flour, sugar, and lard. Yoh didn't had no refrigerator. Soh when yoh buy lard, that was to fry fish. Yoh buy yoh fish, clean dem and fry dem, and put dem in somet'ing whe' ants can't bother dem. Back then yoh put yoh table foot in a li'l can wid oil and water soh ants won't climb on de table.

That li'l dollar I geh every week from Mr. Griffith and de li'l odds and ends Mrs. Griffith gi'e meh help through de tough time. Then when pear (avocado) and mango was een, I went up deh and pick mango and pear foh dem. And when I went up deh, deh gi'e meh breakfast. . . I geh meh fresh cow milk and bread.

Mr. Petrus is de man who use to drive de plough foh Mr. Griffith. He had a team of mules, 'bout four big strapping mules. De plough was a double t'ing, a double shank or wha' yoh call it. Soh when de plough man, Mr. Petrus, mek a cut, he cut two banks one time.

I mention Lenard Schrader, "Chooksen," before. Well, he use to ride a donkey from Grove Place to Bag to work. One day he seh, "yoh want to see a joke?" I seh, "yes." He seh, "I gon tell this jackass . . . I gon pleh merengue and tell he to dance Spanish." Then he tickle de donkey wid his heels and de donkey kickup and poop and went on. When I see how de donkey carry on, I seh "man, do it again." Because I didn't believe it was real . . . dat he could just talk to de donkey and de donkey goh on like that. Sometimes he'll be on de donkey and de donkey walking quite easy. Then all of a sudden yoh hear "boop boop boop", and de donkey start ah sheet ah kicking up. An' I and de other fellows deh deh bussing we belly wid laugh. Matter of fak, all de older boys had a donkey. "Feni," Leroy, Gustave, and of course "Chooksen." I was de only one who had to walk from St. George to Bag toh work. When we goin' up de road in de marnin', I seh to Chooksen, "Chooksen, mek de donkey dance merengue." And he'd do somet'ing and de donkey would start to perform.

Now leh meh tek yoh back to Concordia. Not East Concordia, bu' de one near Harden.

While living wid meh mother at Concordia, I met a man name William "Willi" Matthews. He was 'bout to be married and ask meh toh cut some coconut branches foh him. He want to mek a wedding tent near he house. I cut de branches for him, he mek de tent, got married, and we became very close. He mek cart wheels and I help him mek dem. I ripped big tipet trunks apart. He mek slabs from dem, seh about two to three-and-a-half inches thick. These was wha'was called de fellas. Deh was cut in pieces and form a circle. We used gri-gri to mek de spokes.

Later Mr. Matthew rent some land in Bag from Mr. Griffith and I went up deh wid him toh help work de land. We start out plantin' tania and extended to sugarcane. But then it had soh much rat and mongoose, deh use toh destroy de sugarcane dem. Toh combat dat, we plant cassava in de bank between de cane. We want de mongoose to turn from de cane to de cassava. Well ah tell yoh, deh shell de cassavas, I mean eat dem and left only de shell. Deh do de same t'ing wid de sweet potato.

And I didn't know that tania could bloom. Yes, man, nice purple flowers. And dese tania use toh grow tall. When yoh stand up in dem, deh cover yoh. An' I plant lettuce, eggplant, and in noh time deh come right up 'cause de land was fertile.

Later I went toh live wid Mr. Matthew and his wife, Miss Florence. Mr. Matthew was also a fisherman and I help him mek his fish pots. We use black sage, black wiss, basket hoop, wild cane, tambrand twigs, and grape wood toh mek fish pot. Bu' we also mek dem from ol' trans-Atlantic cable wire. Meh job was to straighten de wire, measure dem, and have dem ready foh Mr. Matthew toh mek fish pot. We also use de white wiss foh fish pot rope. A man name Lawrence pick de wiss 'round La Vallee, mek de rope, and sell dem, $1.80 foh a ten-fathom rope.

Mr. Matthew had a bateau and three fishermen helpers: Allick McBean, Herman Pedro, and a man call

Hungry pelicans cooping chow.

Photo by David Morales

"Ah ha! Ah ketch e! Ah ketch e!"

"Man" Jones. Dese helpers tek turn goin' to sea wid Mr. Matthew. Only three of us went on a particular day: Mr. Matthew, de captain; one of de men, and meh. I was a regular. Anytime de boat pull out, I was in deh. In dem days deh was noh such t'ing as outboard motor. We use oars toh push de boat. One man was middle de boat wid two oars. He and Mr. Matthew tek turns pulling de oars. I had de bow oar. I was like de driver. I sit in de front of de boat, guiding it wid a smaller oar. An' Mr. Matthew sit in de back, bu' relieve de middle man on de two oars when he geh tired. When we done haul pot, we put up a piece of cloth for de sail to run off de wind comin' een.

We left home early foreday marnin' 'bout three o'clock, and push off from de bayside 'round four o'clock, and geh back between eleven and twelve o'clock. One marnin' Miss Florence mek one ah dem big dum johnny cake wid fat pork in it. She cut it in four, put it in a calabash, and gi'e toh meh toh walk wid foh when we hauling pot, toh eat somet'ing before we come een 'cause we doh geh hungry. Now wile deh hauling pot, I gah to keep up on de oar. Two of dem hauling pot, I keepin' up de boat toh de sea. Ev'ry now and then, I shove meh hand in de calabash and break off piece of johnny cake. Soon de whole big dum johnny cake gone. Not a piece leave in de calabash. Mr. Matthew use to call meh "Charlie." He seh, "Charlie, pass de t'ing deh wid de johnny cake." Now, I know it ain' gah noh mo' johnny cake. Bu' I still pu' down meh head in de boat an' seh "ah looking, man, I lookin', meh head deh down deh lookin'." When I geh tired lookin', I sit up. Bu' this time meh ain' sayin' a word. He seh, "Man ah tell yoh, pass de johnny cake, gi'e meh!" I seh, "It ain' gah noh johnny cake." He seh, "Wha' yoh mean it ain' gah noh johnny cake?" "De johnny cake done," I seh. He then lets meh to know, "well, yoh know yoh done eat da johnny cake. Yoh ain' gah noh mo' food toh geh today." Me ain' argue wid he 'cause I respect he.

We finally geh home and Mr. Matthew went goh sell de fish. Bu' he ain' sell all. He pu' some aside, da wha' he gon use foh de house. Now when he come back, he clean fish and he cook. He use to cook de li'l k'tie, docta fish, goat fish, and t'ing. He cook docta fish and fungi. Bu' he ain' leave none foh me. Before, when he finish cook he would seh, "Charlie, yoh food deh deh" or somet'ing. Bu' he ain' seh nuttin'. Soh, I wait 'til Miss Florence, his wife, come. Da day she reach home 'bout four o'clock. When she reach, I went to pull out de haus out de cart and I tell her . . . I seh, "Miss Florence, meh ain' geh noh food yoh know." She seh, "Wha' yoh mean, yoh ain' geh noh food?" I seh, "Well dis marnin' when we been out toh sea, I eat de johnny cake and Mr. Matthew seh he hope I know da was meh food foh de day." "Boy!" she seh, "yoh eat off da whole johnny cake?" "Yes," I seh, "I been hungry." Then she went to cook and she fry fish and johnny cake and gi'e meh. Miss Florence use to tek care ah meh. I remember de first pair ah bag-drawers I ever pu' on, she mek dem foh meh. She had noh children. Bu' she was like a second mother toh meh.

I live wid de Matthews from de time I was thirteen years old 'til I was seventeen. In 1936 meh and he break up. How we break up? On Fourth of July of da year (1936), deh had horse racing on de Oval in Frederiksted. An' I went to see de race. One of meh job 'round Mr. Matthew was toh cut grass foh two haus and a donkey. I mek sure that I cut de grass and gi'e de haus and donkey before I left Concrodia, then I went toh town toh see de races. I didn't goh home da night 'cause deh had quadrille dance in town. Yoh know when yoh deh wid yoh friends dem, young boys from de country, yoh come toh town, yoh roaming town and goin' on and t'ing. Yoh know. . . . Well, after de dance over, three o'clock in de marnin', I can't find de crowd, meh friends dem: Leander Trottman, Isaiah Rogers, and Walter Phillips. Soh, I didn't goh home. I stay in town by meh aunt, in "Joe Boysie" (Joseph Samuel) meh uncle room. About ten o'clock de next day when I geh toh Concordia toh Mr. Matthew house, I meet all meh t'ings outside on de bench whe' we do carpentry. Meh li'l trunk wid meh clothes, meh dishpan wha' I eat in, and meh knife, fork, and spoon was all deh. Mr. Matthew ask meh whe' I been and I tell he. He seh, "whe' yoh sleep?" And I seh, "in town to meh aunt." Then he seh, "see yoh t'ing dem deh. Yoh could goh back whe' yoh come from!"

Mr. Matthew gi'e me de belief dat he had a li'l bankbook foh meh, dat he was saving a li'l money foh meh. Soh I ask he 'bout de bankbook. He seh, "man, yoh ain' gah a t'ing in it." Soh meh ain' argue. . . . I had nuttin' to argue 'bout. Yoh see, I wasn't on pay. I live wid he, do all de work he tell meh toh do. I eat and sleep in he house, he buy meh a pair ah shoes an' some clothes. An' I use toh goh toh church wid he. An' then. . .when he tell meh I ain' had a t'ing deh, noh money in de bank, all I do was cry. Because when t'ings like dat happen to meh, I use toh think dat if meh father was alive dis would not have been happenin' toh me.

Meh father died in 1929. After his death I had live wid meh uncle "Joe Boysie" foh about a year. So when Mr. Matthew pu' meh out, I went back to live wid him in town bu' not foh long. One Sunday foreday marnin', he come

58

wid a piece of neck pork he had geh on Lagoon Street whe' meh aunt use to butcher pork. I was asleep and he wake meh up. "Tek this piece of pork," he seh. "Pu' it in de ironpot; pu' de ironpot in de coalpot, an' pu' de calabash over it." Dat was to avoid ants. De house had holes in de floor. I use toh sleep on de floor on one of dem big ol' sugar bag, dem big crocus bag. Somehow or de other a cat come in de house and went wid de pork. De Sunday marnin' meh uncle come back—he was a man about 6' 3" or more. Soh he come. . . . He had bridle rein hangin' up on de right-hand side of de door (he liked haus). He seh, "whe' de pork?" I seh, "it deh deh." He seh, "look foh it." I tek up the calabash. . . noh pork. Bu' I can see on de floor whe' de cat haul it. And wid dat he tek down de bridle rein from de door and start beatin' me. (I still gah de mark dem.) Every time he fire, I pu' up meh hand. When I t'ink he beat meh enough an' I couldn't stand any more, I charge he. He had de door hook on top and when I ram against he, de whole door went. He kafoon outside and I on top of he. When I geh up, I ran like hell down Pan Bush to meh aunt house, bu' she wasn't home. I sit down on de step. A woman by de name of Cyntia Forbes on her way from church see meh deh on de step, meh undershirt full of blood, and ask meh wha' happen toh meh. I start toh tell her and I faint. She mek some tea and gi'e meh, and I sit down deh 'til meh aunt come. When meh aunt come, before I could tell her anyt'ing, Cyntie tell her wha' happen toh meh. When she come in de yard she went straight foh her tammyhawk bill [canebill], tie a piece cloth 'round her waist, and shub de bill between de cloth behind her and went after meh uncle. Somebody tell he she was coming and he ran foh he life.

59

During his early years, James Richards moved "from press to desk," living between family and friends. He often roamed the bayside, the countryside, and streets of West End; sometimes not going home for days—in his words until his clothes "was tear-up." He later matured, learned auto mechanics, and operated a truck.

Richards spent thirty-three years away from his native St. Croix. He went to St. Thomas in the mid-forties and worked for the U.S. Navy as an auto mechanic in Sub Base and on Water Island. In 1951, he moved on to Puerto Rico where he worked in the late Munoz Marin's (Governor of Puerto Rico) "Operation Bootstrap" program, making rum bottles and cardboard boxes for export. He rose from mechanic helper to supervisor before he left for Indiana a few years later. "When I got to Indiana," he said, "I went toh an employment agency looking foh a mechanic job but all deh offer meh was a dishwasher job. I seh no, and continue toh look. I end up workin' in a glue factory foh $2.25 an hour. Deh tek cattle hide and de skin from buffalo head and boil toh a high temperature toh mek glue. Loads and loads of cattle and buffalo skin use toh come toh da place. An' it use toh stink like hell! Meh job was toh goh under de cellar and pick up da old grease. It look like deh had da old grease foh over ten years, waitin' foh meh toh come clean it up."

"I was deh only a few days when I notice that deh had signs on de bathroom dem saying BLACKS ONLY and WHITES ONLY. This day I went an' I peep in one, then I peep in de other and de boss see me. 'Puerto Rico,' he said (he use to call meh 'Puerto Rico' because I tell him that I had just come from Puerto Rico), 'what are you doing there?' 'Well,' I seh, 'dis bathroom says BLACKS ONLY and de other says WHITES ONLY and I wan' toh see if there is any difference inside.' 'Oh,' he said, 'if you are around here long enough you'll find out!' 'Don't worry,' I seh, 'I am not going toh be around here long enough toh find out.'

"I seh toh mehself, 'yeh, ah soh ahyoh stand down yah?' De first chance I geh, I quit de job and head foh New York. Noh sah, none ah dis 'Blacks Only, Whites Only' business wid me!"

For some youths, as in James Richards' time, West End Fish Market is the "lime".

Cyprian Vicars

MEMORIES OF ST. PATRICK'S

December 24, 1994, began as an ordinary day for me. But halfway through the day, I ran into a story, or, rather, a story ran into me.

Got up at 5:30 a.m. Prayed. Showered. Breakfasted. About 7:30, I put some books and T-shirts in my pick-up truck and headed west to Frederiksted for a business day at Vendors Plaza. Although a ship was in, there was no steady flow of tourists, just a dribbling now and then. Nevertheless, it was Christmas Eve and my spirit was relatively high. I was looking forward to Midnight Mass at St. Ann's Church at Barren Spot. As a member of the choir, I took the opportunity between customers to turn on a few tunes in my head in preparation for the nearly 2,000 years' celebration of Christ's birth.

Just about noon, I saw a familiar face, with sunglasses, under a broad-rim straw hat, a "Paiewonsky hat," named after the late governor Ralph Paiewonsky. It was his "trademark" years ago and the name stuck. The person was Cyprian Vicars and he was accompanied by his wife, Josie. They were visiting from Stone Mountain, Georgia. Visitors, yes, but visitors with deep roots in St. Croix. "Hey man!" he said, as we shook hands, "Gwenie (Lucas) told me you would be here. I need a couple of your books."

Vicars is a retired chief warrant officer who served in the United States Navy and Army. As a former military person myself, we easily got into a little "military talk." Soon the conversation shifted to Frederiksted, old-time West End. "This is good old-time stuff, mehson!" I thought. "Bring it yah!" Pointing to the water in front of us, he said, "Right there. . . when I was a boy, I used to swim right around there, me and other guys from St. Patrick's School."

"Tell me 'bout it man. Tell me 'bout it," I said. And there began the walk back into the '40s and '50s as told to me by Vicars.

I was taught by Belgian nuns. From kindergarten to the twelfth grade, there were Mothers: Ermine, Esther, Matthew, Gonzales, Alban, Diphna, Adele, Leona, Luciana, Christian, Xavaria, and Florentina. Mother Florentina was the superior or principal in my early years. Later Mother Constantina became the principal. She was one of the most beautiful nuns I have ever seen. When I first saw Mother Constantina, I thought she was an angel from heaven. She was so pretty. She was indeed very beautiful and a very sweet nun too.

Mother Constantina played the organ and piano and directed the choir. Back in those days, everything was done by the numbers. When Mother Constantina clapped her hands at the end of recess, you stopped dead in your tracks—not a single movement. When the bell rang and she clapped her hands again, that was the signal to get into formation. And at the sound of the piano, with Mother Constantina at the keyboard, we marched like little soldiers into school, not a sound, not a murmur.

After lunch, my buddies and I would go behind Fort Frederik for a swim. These were fellows such as Leopold Rodriguez, Epifanio Felix, Roosevelt Heyliger, and a few others. The area behind the Fort was known as "Target Wall." We had no such things as bathing suits. We jumped into the water naked as newborns and had a grand time.

My mother was working at Frederiksted Hospital. One day when I got home she noticed that there was sand in my shoes and wanted to know where I had been. I said that I was walking down the beach and the sand got in my shoes. But she then saw the remnants of salt on my face and arms. Yet I swore up and down that I was not in the seawater and was just walking on the beach. "If I ever catch you down there in that water," she said, "you know wha' you goin' get." But I went ahead anyway. Every day at noontime, I was in the water with my schoolmates. However, we had a rule that we went to the beach as a group and we returned as a group. No member of the group could leave by himself to go back to school. If one tried to leave, the others threw sand on him, forcing him back into the water to get the sand off his skin. One day I was trying to leave because I had a feeling that my mother was going to come and check on me, and I wanted to leave before she got there. But everytime I tried to sneak off, Roosevelt Heyliger, now known as "The Tackler," kept throwing sand on me. Then I saw a pair of trousers floating out to sea. Heliger asked if they were mine and I said no. My trousers had a brown belt and those trousers had a green belt. Little did I know that what I thought was a belt was my necktie! In those days we wore the green necktie with the initials "SPS" (St. Patrick's School). Somehow the necktie had come out of the pocket and was wrapped around my trousers. It looked to me like it was a pair of trousers with a green belt, but it was actually a necktie. When I realized what was happening, I thought now my mother would catch me for sure. I couldn't leave because Heyliger kept throwing sand on me and now I had no trousers to put on. ["It was cocobay pon top ah yaws," trouble upon trouble.] But Heyliger who was a better swimmer than I went out there like a fish and retrieved my trousers. I breathed a little easier. But my troubles weren't over. So now I was saying to myself, "How the heck am I going to go back to school in a pair of wet trousers?" I had to get back to school. And so I took the trousers, squeezed out the water, put them on, and went back to school, sat in my desk, and prayed to God that the teacher didn't call on me for anything. Because she would have noticed my wet trousers. And that meant going to the office. Which meant my mother would have known and that also would have meant another whipping. But thank God I was lucky that day.

When boys such as my buddies and I got together, we were always challenging one another to perform some feat. There was always a a test to determine who could run the fastest, swim the farthest, or dive the best. The "Target Wall" beach area was one of the battle grounds. There were two narrow concrete planks, one higher than the other, which extended over the water. If you could climb to the top of the high one and dive into the sea, clearing the second one, you were okay. Most of us could do it. But there was a girl named Gloria who was always trying to compete with us. Whatever we did, she also tried to do. One Saturday morning, Gloria tried to perform this diving feat. But it was fatal. She jumped off the first plank, failed to clear the second and crashed head-on, breaking her neck. It was very tragic. A curtain of sorrow fell over the town. It took a long time for the people of Frederiksted to get over Gloria's death.

At St. Patrick's, Mother Alban, my fourth-grade teacher, was the most feared nun at school. She was quick with the leather strap. As you stumbled—didn't do your work or were out-of-line—you could expect to get a taste of Mother Alban's leather strap. She didn't fool around. As you slipped, you got it.

Mother Adele was the sweetest of them all. She taught me in the sixth grade. During that time, I had great aspirations of becoming a religious brother. But Mother Adele tried to encourage me to become a priest instead. I didn't want to become a priest because to become a priest, one had to go to college. And at that time I didn't think that I had the "smarts" or the inclination to go to college. I know I didn't have the money. Yet Mother Adele tried her best to get me to become a priest rather than becoming a religious brother.

In the seventh grade, Mother Leona taught me book-keeping, shorthand, and so on. I think with my work, or Mother Leona's work with me, these courses were the building blocks, the foundation from which I stepped out into the world of work.

Which nun at St. Patrick's School would you say stands out in your memory above all the others, and why?

That would be Mother Christian. She was the kind of person with whom you established a love-hate relationship. She could embarass you in a minute, but you loved her anyway. Let me tell you a little story. In those days the boys had to play in one playground and the girls in another. And the boys couldn't cross over to the girls' territory and the girls couldn't cross over to the boys' domain. Yes, a kind of separate-but-equal arrangement. Well, somehow I found myself in the girls' playground. You see, there was this one girl that I used to like. Her name was Idolia Belardo, Johnny Belardo's daughter. She was the love of my life, and every time I got a chance, I would be over in the the girls' playground, talking to Idolia. One day Mother Christian caught me. When recess was over, we marched into school. But as customary, we prayed before sitting down to our desks to begin work. While praying, I looked up and saw Mother Christian's face, red as a bee ready to sting. As soon as we said "Amen," she tore into me like a bullet. WHAM! "Cyprian Vicars," she said, "never, never...you understand me...never must I ever see you talking to that Puerto Rican girl again!" I was so embarrassed, I wanted the earth to open up and swallow me.

Another event comes to mind. Mother Christian also taught Spanish. She would write some Spanish verbs on the blackboard and have us conjugate them in the various tenses: present, past, and future. That day she told us to conjugate a word in the future tense. Not paying close attention, I conjugated the word "future." I wrote "future, futurer, and futurest." When she graded the papers, she said "There is someone in here who went so far as to conjugate the word "future" I felt so bad. I was praying that she wouldn't call my name.

But the thing that stands out most in my mind about Mother Christian, and I give her great credit for it, was the importance that she placed on morality, on marriage— the sanctity of marriage and growing up to become good solid citizens of high moral character. And I believe that if it were not for Mother Christian...I can't say for sure...but she brought home to me the idea of the sanctity of marriage and why it was important to marry a woman, rather than just live with her. She brought that home to me. And I would say that in my adult life, of all the people other than my family, other teachers (nuns), priests, I think that Mother Christian had the most profound impact on my life. It was not only what she said, but just her look of disgust about people who were living together and not married. She would say things like she had never seen her parents kissing themselves up. Or things like: "There is no gentleman after six o'clock."

Of course she said much more about morality than I can remember. Religion was our first class and during that time she spoke about marriage, about having respect for one's self, having respect for yourself as a young man or young woman, having respect for women, the dignity of womanhood, the dignity of motherhood. These were the kinds of things she stressed, and they have stayed with me all this time. She really put the fear of God in us about divorce. That was a terrible thing to happen. She said that in any marriage, there were trials and errors but there is a give and take, and marriage was forever, until death. Mother Christian had us convinced that if we got married and later divorced, we were going straight to hell. That's how strong she was. Marriage was an important sacrament and church laws governing marriage had to be obeyed.

Additionally, she brought to the classroom lessons on etiquette. A gentleman should never extend his hand first to a lady—the woman must always extend her hand first, and then the man could extend his. She told us that back in Belgium a man had extended his hand to a woman first and the woman spat in his hand.

Who was Father Knoll?

Father Knoll came to St. Croix as a very young priest.

He said he was 28 years old when he arrived. However, my ealiest experience with Father Knoll was in the early 40s when he came regularly to our home in New Town to bring Holy Communion to my great-grandmother. It was the highlight of my day whenever he came, because that meant that I would ride to school with him in his car after he had given her Holy Communion. And I would feel good about the ride all day.

Father Knoll was here for about four years. When he was ready to go back to the United States, the people cried and cried. The whole church was in tears. Everyone knew him and he was loved by everyone. They called him the "baba" priest.

Father Knoll was replaced by Father Berria. He was the priest who went around town and the country on horse-back, visiting his parishioners. The name of the horse was "Ice Cream" and was believed to have been a race horse before it went into the ministry. The people often tried to compare Father Berria with Father Knoll.

"I know Father Knoll would not have done that."

"If Father Knoll was here, he would have done so and so."

"I don't care who they bring. They can't wear Father Knoll shoes!"

They were so attached to Father Knoll. He was gone for about four years and returned when I was in the fifth grade. I was a little disappointed at first when he returned because he didn't seem to recognize me. And if he did, he didn't show it. The priests had a 1949 Dodge. If Father Knoll passed my house ten times a day, he'd honk his horn, and my mother or my great-grandmother would come out and wave to him.

At this point Father Knoll was the Superior or the priest in charge of the church and the school. We were now getting to be big boys and naturally we sometimes stepped out of line. And when we did, he corrected us and we didn't like it one bit. Nevertheless—I didn't know about the other boys—but there was still much love and respect in my heart for the man.

Father Knoll was one of the chief movers, if not the chief mover himself, behind the construction of St. Joseph's Church at Mt. Pleasant. When I was in the ninth grade, a group of boys (including myself) from St. Patrick's sometimes went to Mt. Pleasant to pitch in with the work of building the church. Father Knoll was always there doing carpentry, mixing mortar to make cement blocks, and other work. That's the kind of priest he was. He was not a man with just words—he was an action man.

In 1956, when I was getting ready to leave for the Army, Father Knoll was at Holy Cross Church in Christiansted. I went to see him and found him under a car changing the oil. Thirty years later, we met again at St. Alphonso's Villa, his retirement home in Jacksonville, Florida. He was so happy to see us (my wife Josie and I) as we were to see him. We visited the graves of Father Berria and other priests who had served in the Virgin Islands. Later we checked into a Newsmyner Beach restaurant. We were only seated for a short while when a waitress came up to Father Knoll and asked what he'd like to drink. "I'll take a rubroi [Rob Roy] straight up, with a twist of lime," said Father Knoll. "Cyprian," he added, "what are you

Father Mark Knoll and Josie and Cyprian A. Vicars
Newsmyner Beach Restaurant, Florida.

having?" I was a bit stunned. "Father Knoll," I said, "as one of your altar boys at St. Patrick's, who would have thought that forty years later, I would be here on a beach in Florida having cocktails with you!"

Cyprian Vicars did not spend all of his time jumping in and out of the sea off "Target Wall" in Frederiksted when he was not in a St. Patrick's School classroom. He had several apprenticeships with elder tradesmen. He was with the Alexander Benjamin blacksmith shop near the cemetery and "Bass" John blacksmith shop in Foster, until an uncle warned him that there was no guarantee that a willful horse wouldn't crap on his head while shoeing its rear hooves or perhaps stomp on him then take a good bite out of his behind. He later tried tinsmithing with Henry Francis of Smithfield who took him to Bethlehem Sugar Factory on Saturday mornings where Vicars was "fascinated by all that machinery." But he liked best going to Bethlehem on Fridays. That was the day he could stuff his belly with lechon (roast pig) from Carmelo. At the insistence of his grandmother, he also had a taste of carpentry. Vicars also had a little experience in electronics with Heinrich Nielsen who operated a radio repair shop in Frederiksted.

After graduation from St. Patrick's School in 1953, Vicars worked for McFarlane Construction Company as a bookkeeper for $18.00 a week. He moved on to the Virgin Islands Corporation (VICORP) at Bethlehem Sugar Factory when his boss and former police sargeant Herman Sarauw refused to give him a raise "because he didn't think I needed one." At Bethlehem he received a hefty sum of $40.00 weighing sugarcane at the factory scalehouse with Marcial Morales. When the sugarcane season was over, he worked in the accounting section as a bookkeeper under the supervision of Wally Ross.

The old people say, "'tis because of ungratefulness mek e gah cocobay." But Cyprian Vicars is not an ungrateful person, far from it. When he learned from Father Knoll that Mother Christian (Sister Mary Schodts) and Mother Constantina (Sister Mary Augusta Lumbeek) were still living, he immediately began to make plans to go to Belgium.

I wanted to visit the place which has produced such people, who would leave their families and friends and go far away home, knowing that they might never see them again. But most of all, I wanted to go to Belgium to personally express my gratitude to those nuns for the great sacrifice that they made in coming to St. Croix to teach us. Because if it were not for them, we might not have been what we are today. I really wanted to say thanks to them for helping us to make responsible citizens of ourselves. You'll hear some people say, "Oh, the Army, the Navy, or the Marines did so and so for me." Well, I want to tell you that the military didn't do a thing for me. I got my training, my discipline, from St. Patrick's

School, not the military. I was a better man in the Navy and Army because of St. Patrick's School, not the other way around.. And of course credit must be given to the parents of my wife Josephine, Reuben and Margaret Ludwig, to my mother Henrietta A. Williams, grandmother Anna Williams, and godmother Rebecca Benjamin. Those dear hearts and gentle people made it all happen, by making the sacrifices necessary to send us to Catholic school. They were people of vision who saw early on the benefits to be derived from a Catholic education.

In early June 1994, Cyprian and his wife Josie left Atlanta for Belgium where they had a very warm, happy reunion with the people who helped shape their lives (Josie is also a product of St. Patrick's School).

Mother Christian was waiting for us. She was so happy, she embraced us and the tears—tears of joy—rolled down our cheeks. We talked about the old times and I reminded her of the time I tried to conjugate the word "future" and we had a good laugh about that. We also saw Mothers Constantina, Borgia, and Letitia who had taught my sister Mary. We not only expressed our gratitude to these nuns but also to all the other nuns who had touched our lives in a special way and have gone to their eternal reward.

On July 31, 1979, the curtain fell on the twenty-three year military career of Cyprian Vicars. It was a happy day. There was a retirement ceremony in his honor and his family was at his side.

I was especially happy that my mother could be with me. Because without her guidance and sacrifices, I could not have made it to that point in my life. I thought of the time in school when I wanted a camera so badly. It cost $39.95 but she did not have the money. It was more than she made in a whole month working at the hospital. And yet she found a way. She sent me to Schade Apothecary to ask him if he would trust her with the camera, that she would pay him a little each month until the debt was satisfied. Mr. Schade said yes, it was okay, and I got my camera. My mother died in January 1994 and I thank God for her. If it were not for her and St. Patrick's, I would not be what I am today.

Cyprian Vicars, Mother Christian, Josie Vicars and Mother Borgia, Louvain, Belgium.

Frederiksted's own Sylvester "Blinky" McIntosh of Blinky and The Road Masters keeping Quadrille and Quelbe' alive.

WEST END FISH MARKET

Frederiksted has it all: Buddhoe Park, where Freedom was born; St. Gerard's Hall, home of quadrille and quelbe; and West End Fish Market, soul of Frederiksted. And Frederiksted is the soul of St. Croix. There are few places on St. Croix that are as special to many Crucians as West End Fish Market. Seven days a week, Fish Market teems with life. There are fishermen going to sea and fishermen returning from sea. And the folks wait, wait with their bags, pans, and other containers for the fishermen to start selling. Sometimes 'tis larrum when fishermen pull up their boats with loads of fish, not to mention jacks. When jacks are in, people go wild, swarming over the boats like honey bee looking for nectar, shouting their bids:

"Gi'e meh five pound ah jacks!"

"Ah wan' ten pound. Come, man. Yoh stirrin' toh slow. Meh ha' foh goh cook!"

"An' meh wan' twenty pound. Pu' all in yah, dis bucket."

"Bu' whe' she ah goh. . . . She noh see me yah? She jus' come an' she bore right een. Ah feel like ah could buss she one calabash in she head, bu' meh 'fraid e bruk. Meh noh gah nuttin' else foh pu' meh fish."

Moreover, whenever there is a boat with kingfish, bluefish, red snapper, and other big fish, it can be even worse.

"Ah wan' dis one, da' one, an' all ah dem deh."

Paul Horsford, Arthur Edney, and Isidro Griles of Blinky and The Road Masters.

"Wait ah minute.... Woman, yoh noh see yoh ah 'tandup 'pon meh foot? Seh excuse!"

"O'...pardon meh. Noh, meh noh been see yoh foot 'cause yoh had um under fohmeh foot."

"Noh talk stupid. Yoh walk 'pon meh foot an' mash um. How yoh gon' see um when yoh come flyin'...yoh head high high pon' yoh neck like gaulin bird. Bu' yoh eye deh fasten 'pon de fish dem, like whelks 'pon rock."

"Come on, Mr. Man. Ah wan' meh fish. Gi'e meh fish. Ah been yah since marnin'."

"Ah wonder whe' she gwine. Woman, move yohself from in front ah meh! Yoh come late an' wan' toh goh hurry. If yoh t'ink yoh goin' geh any fish yah tohday before meh, yoh lie."

Keeping Quadrille and Quelbe' alive, Wayne "Bully" Petersen of "Bully" and The Kafooners.

Bottom left to right: Lloyd Thomas (Pedico), Emmett Richards, Wilfred Allick, Jr. (Bomba), Top left to right: Headless steel player, Isidro Griles, Vivian Charles, David Ferris and Raymond Richards ("Hoofer") of "Bully and The Kafooners."

But people go to Fish Market not only to buy fish. They go there to "cool out," to talk politics and sports and melee, and anything and everything under the sun. If something is going to take place on St. Croix, you can be sure to hear about it first at Fish Market. The winners of the governor and senate races are announced at Fish Market long before the elections are over and the ballots counted. Fish Market is also a cultural market where folks gather to sell bush tea, sorrel, benye, pate, souse and kallaloo, and a "booku" of other cultural goods and goodies.

One Saturday, I met Olivia Andrews, Calvin Perkins, and Kai Lawaetz at the Fish Market and joined in their morning talk as they went about selling various produce and food items. I came in on Lawaetz's story.

80

"The little fellow could speak very little English. One day I sent him to a store in Frederiksted. 'Jose,' I said. 'I want you to go to town [Frederiksted] to the store near the Post Office. Get me a hard tooth brush and a tube of tooth paste. Do you understand?' 'Yeh, Mr. Kai, yeh sir,' he reply. And he was on his way from Little La Grange. (When Jose arrive at the store, it happened that my sister was also there getting a few things.) Calling the storekeeper by name, Jose made his request. 'I wan' a hard toothache an' a soft tooth brush foh Mister Kai,' he said. And the little store exploded with laughter."

Let me tell you a different "toothpaste" story as was told by my aunt, Elvina Thomas, in *Kallaloo* (1991):

Around 1919 the American Red Cross began distributing toothpaste in the schools on St. Croix. One day, Mr. Wilson, head teacher of La Vallee School, got his supply and on the same day when school was over, he gave the toothpaste to the children. They were so happy, they ran home with it to show their parents. The following day when the children return to school, like a good teacher Mr. Wilson began asking them how they like the toothpaste. 'Fredo,' he said to one of the boys. 'Will you tell the class how you enjoyed the toothpaste. Do you like it better than using ashes to brush your teeth?' Fredo did not respond but a girl volunteer to speak for him. But before she could say anything about the toothpaste, she began laughing. 'Why are you laughing?' ask teacher Wilson. 'Well,' said the girl. 'Fredo ain' know anyt'ing 'bout de toothpaste. His gran'mother eat it. Dis marnin' I heard Fredo gran'mother call out toh meh auntie. She seh "Tanto, tanto!" Well, leh meh tell yoh somet'ing. Well, Fredo bring home ah lozenge yah las' night, e been soh soft, ah noh eben had toh chew e self.'

And while I still had the floor, I told another story.

It took place at Estate Fredensborg during the 40s. In those days the coal pot was quite common. One day a neighbor had not one but two coal pots in action. But when the fish and fungi was almost ready, she discovered that she didn't have a drop of vinegar to make the gravy for the fish. She turned to her son and told him to go to Miss "Vero," a woman who live several houses away, and ask for a little vinegar so that she might complete her cooking. But the boy stop on the way to play three-whole-marble under a Taman tree. By the time the game was over he had only a vague idea of what his mother had said. He considered running back home to clear up the message. But that was too risky. That was trouble. That was nothing but a whipping and so he forgot about it and ran to Miss Vero's house. 'Miss Vero,' he said out of breath. 'G-o-o-d a-f-t-e-r-n-o-o-n. . .meh. . .meh m-o-t-h-e-r seh if yoh gah any winddigar to please send li'l foh her."

Perkins changed the subject.

"Mehson, this drought is killing us. If we don't get some rain soon, I don' know what we are goin' to do."

Andrews chimed in.

"Look, look," pointing at the sea. "See the weather birds. They are in so close and there are so many of them. It remind me of the time just before Hurricane Hugo. You remember what 'Fungi' (Alvin James) had said on Doc James Radio Talk Show? He said that weather birds were seen hovering over the sea in many areas and that was a sure sign that the hurricane was going to hit St. Croix."

I added a little piece.

According to Frankie Pete (Frank Petersen), when the weather is so hard that the grass turns brown and the cracks in the earth multiply and through it all the flamboyant blooms, bright and lovely as they are, watch out! A storm is in the making.

Perkins jumped in.

"Well, I certainly don't want to see another hurricane, but we can sure use some rain, plenty of it. The place is dry as a chip. Comparing to years ago, there has been a big change in the weather. Rain don't fall on St. Croix like it use to. When I was a boy living at St. John, there were several springs shooting up water in the nearby canefields. My sister and I had to carry large kerosene pan of water on our heads from a canefield near the main road to water plants and for other home use. There was a well at Estate Rattan so deep one could not see the bottom. A platform was built 'round the well and water was obtain by a bucket which was lower into the well by a reel."

"Years ago," said Andrews, "when it rain, it rain for hours. It rain 'till the guts came down. In 1936 it was even reported in de newspaper that it rain so much on Frederiksted Northside and the water level was so high that Kai Lawaetz had to swim 'cross Little La Grange gut to get to his house. Do you remember that, Kai?"

"Oh yes," said Lawaetz. "Certainly. Just to give you an example, in 1978 during Hurricane Frederick, there was eleven feet of water in Little La Grange gut."

The conversation turned to Creque Dam. In what year was it built, I asked?

"About 1925," replied Perkins. "I graduate from Christiansted Junior High School the same year. I got a job with Public Works at Peter's Farm. They had just build the hospital. I was there only a short time when eight of us were send to work on Creque Dam. Those were pickaxe, shovel, and wheelbarrow days, no such t'ing as a backhoe. They paid us ten cent an hour

Leopold Gittens (Pollo) and Douglas Carter.

The boats are in at West End Fish Market (Frederiksted).

but housing was free. We stayed in Frederiksted Monday to Friday and went home on weekends.

"I got my license in 1925 when I was seventeen. Do you remember the model T-Ford? In later years I drove one of them. That's the one which had three pedals: one for the brakes, one for the clutch, and another for reverse. To start it, you had to crank it up with a long cranking iron with a handle. If you didn't know what you were doing, the handle could spin back and hit you on your head or in your face. By the way, I didn't had a spare tire. So when I got a flat, I stop the truck, got out, cut some grass, stuff it in the tire, and drove on it. Oh, yes. I have done it many times."

Lawaetz got in.

"Going back to what you said about the ten cents an hour you received. Back then ten cents had a lot of buying power. In 1896 my father was paid $7.00 a month as an overseer at Estate Granard. It was his first job on St. Croix. He had arrive from Denmark not to long before."

"My father would have been 139 years old today," said Andrews. "He work as an overseer at Estate Low [Lower] Love and was paid 40 cent a day. And every Friday he was given one herring and one pound of cornmeal. In those days there was no such t'ing as eight hours' work. You work 'til the work was done. If a man had to load ten bullcarts of sugarcane on a particular day, he didn't walk out the canefield at 5:00 or 6:00 p.m. He left when the work was done. Pa was also a sugar boiler at Low Love. He told me he use to put a little white lime in the sugar to make it grainy. He also boil sugar with Gatewood James at La Grange factory. They send Gatewood James to Denmark to study Chemistry. But pa was never given that opportunity. He learn on the job. Pa also said that when he bought Mount Washington, he was only making $13.33 a month. He later bought Nicholas."

The conversation shifted.

"In 1932," Perkins recounted, "I work for Fleming as a bus driver, twelve hours a day for $7.00 a week."

Andrews said: "I work as a student nurse in the 30s at Frederiksted Hospital for $10.00 a month and five dollars worth of food. But it was so much food, my mother had to come and get it in her buggy. The buggy use to be loaded down with food, so much food that there was hardly any place left for us to sit. In 1935 two pounds of brown sugar cost only three cents. Two pounds of white sugar was five cents. And you could have gotten a string of fish (that's between five to ten lovely fishes) for seven cents.

"Do you remember when the Puerto Ricans came from Vieques in 1932? My father had over fifty of them working for him. He paid them sixty cents a day to work the land and they really produced. They planted yam and tania at Nicholas and brought it down to Mount Washington by use of a crook on donkeys where they were placed in a storage house.

"But then a whole calabash of yam or tania was five cents. My mother had the best kidney mangoes which she sold one cent for a full calabash. And we had hundreds of goats, pigs, and sheep. We didn't had any refrigerator and so it was carned-goat and carned-pork."

"Speaking of the Puerto Ricans who came to St. Croix in the 30s and the 40s," said Lawaetz, "in the late 40s I had several Puerto Ricans working with me at Little La Grange, planting and reaping things such as yam and other vegetables and fruits. A man by the name of Gonzalez was one of them. We had a very good working relationship. He told me if he found a better job he would leave. I told him 'sure, why not? It is the purpose of man to try to improve his condition in life.' After a year or more, he said

86

he had found another job and was leaving. We parted on good terms. Years later I went into the pineapple business and shipped pineapples to St. Thomas. One day I was in a store making a delivery. When I look up, who should I see but Gonzalez behind the cash register. He was so happy to see me, as I was to see him. When I saw him again a few years later, he had his own store. Gonzalez came to St. Croix as a sugarcane worker but he didn't remain a sugarcane worker for long. He moved up the ladder to a better job. There is a great sense of unity among Puerto Ricans that's lacking among us Crucians. They come together and help each other to move forward. We are too separated. We have our own little this and that, and there lies our weakness as a people."

And we are often unduly hard on one another as is illustrated in the following story:

According to Hubert Hendricks, a Crucian well into his eighties, many years ago there was a very tough canefield "driver." He was ruthless when it came to doing "massa wuk." One day he became very ill and was admitted to Peter's Farm Hospital. This was in the 30s. After he was there several days, he received a visit from the estate massa. "Massa," he said. "Yoh t'ink ah gon' come out ah in yah? Yoh t'ink ah gon' mek it?" The massa remained silent for a moment. Then he spoke. "Yes, man . . . yes, man," he said. "Yoh gon' come out on de third day." Now the massa knew full well that the man was at death's door. "Massa," said the man, "well, watch yah! Leh meh tell yoh, when me geh out ah yah, ah gon' root dem behind in ah da canepiece deh. E' gon' be meh an' dem. E gon' be noh fall back, fallout or goh ahside. E gon' be from bell toh bell an' shell toh shell." But as God would have it, the poor man did not live to keep his promise. He died a few days later.

The talk shifted to politics, then back to old-time St. Croix.

Shark's teeth sharp. But sharp knife guts shark.

Waiting for the pot. What will it be. Fry fish and Johhny cake, or boil-fish and fungi?

Photo by Dr. Dorene E. Carter

Ah big fella, noh true? Otto Gittens and Leslie Myers.

Lt. Governor Derek Hodge comes to Fish Market. Election '94.

Lawaetz had the last word. "My brothers Frits and Erik and I are the last three 'Danish West Indians' on St. Croix, born to Danish parents before the transfer of the Virgin Islands from Denmark to the United States. After we are gone, that breed dies."

And there I was that Saturday morning at West End Fish Market, among nearly 250 years of Crucian experience and enjoying every bit of it. That's why West End Fish Market is so special to Frederiksted and Frederiksted so special to St. Croix because there are many good, solid Crucians around, like Olivia Andrews, Calvin Perkins and Kai Lawaetz.

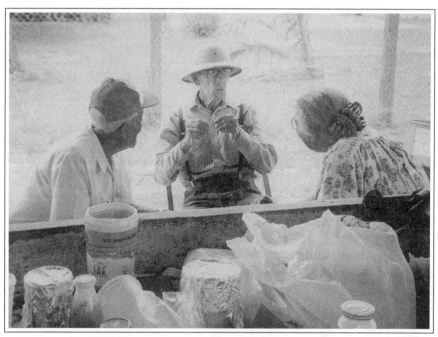

Calvin Perkins, Kai Lawaetz and Olivia Andrews.

MEN OF THE SEA

The old-time fishermen were heroes. Day after day they went to sea in small row boats to hunt for Crucian saltin'. But who remembers these gallant men of the sea? Hardly anyone. They live only in the hearts of their loved ones and a few caring folks. As the old people say, "Wen yoh die, de grass grow before yoh door. An' all de good yoh doh goh down in de hole wid yoh. Only de bad is left behind."

Frederiksted has produced a number of gallant fishermen. Among these are Brother Licrish, Andrew Ferris, Joe Stout, Isaac "Zic" Richards, James Small, Eddy "Tank", Richard and Wilmout Gittens, Joseph Prince, Sam Lewis, Julius Griles, Albert Edwards, Clarence Michael, Gerald and Fritz Fasit, Archie Stevens, Eugene Bennerson, Arthur Smith, and many others. Gerald Facit was a "very businesslike fisherman." It is said that he was very much in love with a girl in Christiansted and so when he went to Christianted to sell fish, he was "tag down" in his suit, hoping to win her perhaps if not words, by appearance.

James Richards remembers the days when Eugene Bennerson, the policeman/fisherman, would pull in the waters near the fish market with fish "toh hurt yoh eye." In those days, the thirties and forties, according to Richards, Bennerson didn't do any selling. His mother, "Mama Pinchie," who lived a stone's throw from the fish market, had the job of selling her son's fish.

Yoh mother may seh, "Boy, tek dis calabash an' goh geh some fish. Tell Mama Pinchie toh sell meh two poun' o' jacks. Da time jacks use' toh be ten cent ah poun'. An' when it gettin' late, yoh might even geh dem foh five cent ah poun'. Now, when yoh goh an' tell Mama Pinchie wha yoh mother seh... 'cause everybody know everybody in town, Mama Pinchie might ask yoh, "Boy! Who is yoh mama?" Yoh may answer meh mother is so an' and so. Mama Pinchie would tek up handsful of jacks an' throw in yoh calabash. An' if she know yoh mother good, de more jacks yoh will geh.

Josephine Bennerson had this to say about Mama Pinchie, her grandmother.

The older people would come and say, "Mama Pinchie! Mama Pinchie! Ah want five pound ah jacks...ah want ten pound...ah want twenty." And Mama Pinchie would say, "ahyoh, noh pu' ahyoh hand 'pon Eugene jacks! Tek um out! Tek um out! Yoh see dem children deh? Dem deh come first. Deh noh gah noh father, deh noh gah noh mother." Meaning there was no one there to look out for them to help them get the fish they wanted and so they came first before anyone else. And if there was a boy or girl who was afraid to open his or her mouth and ask for what they wanted, Mama Pinchie might say to them,: "Yoh boy/yoh gel foh Thant...foh Queenie...wha yoh ah wait 'pon? Yoh wan meh foh tell yoh mama dat yoh 'tandup deh 'til all de jacks done? Come yah, leh meh tek care ahyoh."

She was sweet as sugar. But please don't get her mad. You would hear her voice from fish market to Foundout [Frederiksted Cemetery, nearly half a mile away]!

Mama Pinchie was born Roxelina James. She was a very small baby. And so, because of her small size they called her "Pinchie." As she grew older, Mama, a title of respect, was added. She died in 1953 at the age of 87.

Arthur Smith has been dead for nearly eight years. And yet

he is alive. He lives in the hearts of his daughter and son-in-law, Margarita and Emile Heywood. "My father," said Margarita, "was a master fisherman. Fishing was all he knew. And he did it his entire life. He came to St. Croix from Tortola as a young boy. My father loved the sea. He loved it so much that when he was sent to school, he would sneak off and spend the whole day at the bayside, swimming and fishing. He used old pieces of wire to make fish hooks and for the line he used any twine he could find."

When Smith got older, he bought a boat. At that time there was no outboard motor available to him. Like most fishermen, it was muscle power that pulled the oars that pushed the boat out into the deep and back. Smith made his own fish nets, fish pots (traps), and seine (fishing net). He could always be seen at his home in Concordia, surrounded by fish nets, fish pots, and seine. He was always making or repairing his fishing equipment in preparation for a day at sea.

As a boy, Emile Heywood went on many fishing trips with Arthur Smith. He has some stories to tell.

Early in the morning Arthur would push his boat down in the sea and climb in. He is going fishing but has no bait. He oars up to Sandy Point. He is after sprat. The water is very dirty and the sprat are no way in sight. But Arthur watches the bubbles in the water. He throws his net, pulls in, and there is enough sprat in it to fish for two days. And even without the bubbles appearing in the water, when there seemed to be no signs that the sprat were around, Arthur knew exactly where to cast his net. He had a tremendous feel for the sea, and that came from observing and studying the habits of the fishes. And he knew each month what type of fish he would catch. For example he would say "the kingfish will be biting in October," "in November you should catch plenty jacks," "in December the gars will be running," and so on.

Emile Heywood

Arthur Smith and Archie Stevens would often compete against each other to see who could catch the most fish. They even gave names to their seines. Arthur's seine was *The Saratoga* and Archie's *The Lexington*. They both had their own crew. Clarence Michael ("Li'l Mike") was Archie's headman. When the two boats took off in the morning, you'd hear Li'l Mike say "de current good!" And Archie would lego *The Lexington*. And there would go Arthur with *The Saratoga* after him. So any jacks which would come out of Archie's seine, Arthur would pick them up. But Arthur's seine was much deeper and more finely knitted than Archie's. Hardly any fish could get out. It scraped the bottom of the sea.

Sometimes Arthur caught so many jacks with his seine, it was so heavy, he had to let some escape in order to bring it in. But still there were enough jacks to fill every stall in the fish market. And when "Puelt" (George Henry) or "Phonograph" Brown blew that conch shell to let the people know that "jacks was in," they descended on the fish market like a swarm of pelicans, with pans, pots, baskets, buckets, and crocus bags. Before long you would smell fried fish and johnny cake, the scent coming from those homes in Foster, not too far from the fish market.

Other times Arthur sold his jacks from a truck, going from estate to estate, from Frederiksted to Christiansted. And the by-word was JACKS! JACKS! JACKS! COME GEH YOH JACKS!

But Arthur caught more than jacks and other small fishes. He went after the big ones too, like snapper, kingfish, grouper, barracuda, and many others. And he caught turtles and sold the meat when there were no laws against this in the Virgin Islands. Catching sharks and selling some parts while saving the liver to make shark oil which was used, among other things, to drive away cold, was another favorite pastime. Diving for conch and lobster was another thing he loved to do. And he knew where to find them. Arthur was like a fish in the sea. It was his world and he knew it like the back of his hand.

According to Heywood, there were other mavericks of the sea, like George Henry "Puelt," and Isaiah "Marshall" who didn't own a boat but knew their way around the sea. "Puelt," he said, "was a very good diver and swimmer and was like a sea scout who went ahead of the boat searching the water for jacks. And when he found them he gave the signal and the men in the boat would descend on the spot with the seine. Puelt also dove for conch. When he went down to the bottom of the sea, said Heywood, he brought them up by the armful. And the barracudas darting around him, trying to catch little fishes coming out of the conch shells, were not a problem for him.

Puelt died in the late sixties in the place he loved the best, the sea.

Like Emile Heywood, Doug Nesbitt too has great memories of his mentor, Arthur Smith.

Don Artis, as he was affectionately called, was the consummate fisherman. He did it all. Most fishermen of his era either specialized in pot fishing or bottom fishing. Don Artis worked his pots (fish traps), worked his seine, (even built his own seine), bottom fished, dived for lobster and conch and fished for pelagic fish, i.e. King Fish, Dolphin, Bonito, Tuna, Gar, etc. Don Artis is the only fisherman, in the 30 odd years I was fortunate to learn from him, who could throw a sprat net from any angle in the boat. If a block of sprat was coming toward the boat while the oarsman was backing-up and the sprat changed course, Don Artis would alter his throwing angle to compensate for any shift that school of sprat made. Every throw that he made was near perfect to perfect. When other fishermen were cutting their sprats with knives to make mash (chum) Artis was cutting them with the strength of his thumb and flipping the pieces as the boat drifted along. Being left handed was not a hindrance to Don Artis. He used his left hand with ultimate dexterity.

One morning while we were waiting for the tide to change and the dirty water to run-off in Sandy Point so that we could spot the Jacks, that tastiest of fish that every Crucian so loves, Don Artis decided he had waited long enough, so he told Lloydie Barnes and Skeece Gaskin, who were running the seine boat to cant the pole and round the seine heading to the North. All the fishermen who were Don Artis' peers wanted to know if he was crazy. How could he spot Jacks in this dirty water when nobody else could see. Don Artis explained that he saw bubbles coming to the surface at various intervals, so he knew there were fish under him. When we finally got the seine inland and started to tuck, lo and behold, two boat loads of Jacks was on its way to Frederiksted. Don Artis was the only man who could round bubbles and come up with two boat loads of Jacks!!

Don Artis was a philosopher in his own right. Whenever he did something outstanding, he would attribute it to "Science from Siam." One day after mending the seine and putting it away, Don Artis and his peers sat down to have a few rums and shoot the breeze. The conversation ranged from the sea, to farming, to cattle. Don Artis shocked everybody by stating that he once saw a bull spit. The other fishermen laughed and asked Don Artis if he wasn't sure the bull sneezed or dribbled, but Artis adamantly said over and over again, "no the bull spit." Don Artis was a believer. He went to his grave believing that the bull truly did spit.

Isaiah "Marshall" was a master moko jumbie dancer. He was also noted for his role in the play "David and Goliath." He loved the sea and was a lobster man who knew every lobster hole (cave) around Frederiksted. Marshall had no boat and swam with a crocus bag in which he put his lobsters. He would boil the lobsters caught on the bayside, put them in a big tray which he would then place on his head, going through town selling them. He had a tremendous voice when he shouted "LOBSTER! LOBSTER! Geh yoh boil lobster!" You could hear him from one end of the town to the other.

The old gallant men of the sea have all passed on. They may have been forgotten by some but they live in the hearts of others.

Doug Nesbitt

THE DEATH OF ALBERT EDWARDS

When a bell rings for a funeral, it rings not only for the dead, it rings for the living. It rings as a reminder to us that death is always on the march, coming, coming. And no matter how fast we walk or where we walk in life, it eventually catches up with us. On February 15, 1995, the bell rang at St. Paul's Anglican Church and it was especially for Albert Edwards. His mortal remains laid in a mahogany-colored casket at the rear of the church. And though dead, he appeared to be sleeping so peacefully, in his navy-blue suit, white shirt, and striped tie. He looked like a statesman. Never before had I seen him so handsomely dressed.

There were less than fifty people present. And no senator or other government official showed their faces. It reminds me of the ol' time saying, "When small fry dead, deh noh hear. Bu' when big fish dead, deh hear."

One by one we came up to the casket to see our brother's face for the last time...to say goodbye until we meet again...until the bell rings in our honor. There were murmurings over the body, even touching of the face or arranging the rosary in the hands—little things that women are so accustomed to doing.

"God be wid yoh, yoh hear Albert, 'til ahwe meet ahgain."

"Rest in peace, brother Edwards. Rest in peace."

One women said a little more:

"God bless yoh, mehson. Yoh gone left ahwe yah wid ahwe problems. De Lord be wid yoh."

She then added:

"He was a very kind man. He will give yoh dis an' he will give

Albert Edwards and Osorio Santiago.

yoh dat. I use toh goh by his house when he was sick toh sing an' pray wid him."

The service was very short. One or two songs. And there was none of the "Lord-me-down" sermons like those I have heard before at St. Paul's, to send off brother Edwards. And there was no eulogy to sing praises to the kindness of this man.

Throughout the service, Osorio Santiago, a close friend of Edwards, sat quietly in his seat. When it was over, he hobbled along with his cane in the funeral procession, up the hill. But the pain in his leg was too great, he couldn't get to the cemetery. I had seen him with Edwards before. They had sat together under the shade of the Taman tree near Frederiksted Post Office. It was there that Edwards sold provisions from his land in La Grange several times a week. Everyone knew Edwards and would stop by for a chat or a head of lettuce, tomato, banana, yam, pepper, cassava, tea bush, and so many other things which he grew from the magic of the soil and the love from his hands.

When I caught up with Osorio Santiago, I quickly put the question, "How long have you known Edwards?" "Over forty years," came the reply in Spanish. "And I have been working for him for almost that long. I cut cane, plant cane...plant everything...weed grass and do everything. I don't know if he left me anything...I don't really know. But I worked very hard for him."

Albert Edwards was born on the island of Antigua, British West Indies, on December 15, 1913. But his great-grandmother, Matilda Thomas, was born on St. Croix. His mother brought him to St. Croix when he was about seven years old. They went to Estate Whim where her sister, who also was from Antigua, had previously settled. This was during the early twenties. Whim was a thriving sugarcane plantation with both men and women canefield workers under the management of "Massa" Smith, known for making women workers pregnant, then turning them

102

off the estate when "deh belly start to show." Nevertheless, he took a liking to Edwards and often had him with him on horseback as he rode about the estate checking on his workers. Years later that relationship got Edwards a job driving the estate mule-cart.

Young Edwards oftern walked the long road from Whim to Fountain to see his great-uncle and my great-grandfather, Richard Andreas. Grandfather Richard, who was born around the mid 1800s, would have little talks with his nephew. "Boy, yoh hear wha' meh ah tell yoh.... Ah come yoh ah come...'course t'ing well hard tedey. Bu'...bu'...ah will be dead an' gone bu' e bound foh geh betta. If yoh mek five cent, save two cent. Noh depend 'pon buckra man foh feed yoh. Buy piece ah land when yoh able. Feed yohself. Plant 'nuff ninyam foh yoh yet. Plant! Plant! Plant 'til yoh back hurt yoh. If God dirty (dirt) kin help buckra man pu' money ina foh e pocket, e kin help yoh pu' money ina foh yoh own toh."

As a young man on the move, Edwards ventured into Frederiksted and came under the wings of Eugene Bennerson, a police officer and fisherman, who taught him how to fish. It was perhaps one of the greatest lessons in Edwards' life, for he later fished for a living and had a large number of Frederiksted people as his customers.

There were other jobs too. He worked at Bethlehem sugar factory, lifting 250 lb. bags of sugar, and was a stevedore with Merwin and Company in Frederiksted for a good number of years.

In the thirties and forties, earnings on St. Croix were quite meager. But Edwards saved some of the little money he made, then invested in agricultural land at Prosperity and later La Grange. This gives credence to the saying, "One one full basket." Edwards' investment began a romance with the soil that would last up until the time of his death.

In the cemetery, Edwards was the subject of little conversations. "I am very thankful to da man for what I have become," said Franklin Gumbs. "I served in the Marines and now I am an electrician. Da man deh planted the seeds of discipline and industry in me. When I was about eleven years old, he let me make a little money for myself. He gave me fruits and vegetables to go and sell in town. I used to put them in my little wagon and walk up and down the streets selling. But some boys used to tease me and call me 'mama boy.' When they see me they would shout: 'mama boy, mama boy! See de mama boy deh!' And I would put my hand in my pocket, take out a handful of dollar bills and say, 'see. . .this is de mama boy foh ahyoh.'"

As dirt and rocks fell from the gravediggers' shovels on the casket, another man spoke. "I was surprise toh see soh li'l people in church. Dis man use toh feed nearly de whole town wid fish an' potato an' yam an' soh many other vegetables and fruits." That, I believe, summed up the sentiments of all those present.

Another saying comes to mind. "People will laugh wid yoh when yoh alive. Bu' when yoh dead, deh seh, toh hell wid yoh."

HOW DEH SEH WHA DEH SEH

James Rawlins and Raymond Pedro had a few things in common. Both lived at Grove Place and both were successful businessmen. But they were archenemies. They hated each other with a passion. Pedro was running for a seat in the Municipal Council. And so, he asked one Mr. Francis of Christiansted to introduce him at a political rally at Grove Place one Sunday afternoon. Francis, a quadrille floor master, in addition to being very popular, was very well spoken. Francis knew James Rawlins. However, he did not know that Rawlins and Pedro were bitter enemies. When he was through introducing his good friend Raymond Pedro to the audience, he spotted James Rawlins and immediately began to lavish him with praise. "Mr. James Rawlins," he said: "Stalwart, gentleman of the country, pillar of his community.... Would you please come up here and say a few words on behalf of Mr. Raymond Pedro, champion of labor, worthy servant of the people, great hope for St. Croix!" Rawlins, who was partially blind, took his time getting to the platform. When he was in positiion, he cleared his throat, EH HEM! Then he began: "Well...well...ah gon' tell ahyoh somet'ing. If yoh tek ah jackass an' yoh pu' on ah linen suit 'pon e, buckshoes, pu' ah panama hat 'pon e head, an' bowtie 'roun' e neck, e still ah jackass yoh know. De only difference now, e become ah sophisticated jackass. Good day!"

Years ago the laws against gambling, playing dice, were enforced by the police. If you were caught, you could be arrested and taken to jail. If the person was under age, he (girls were "angels" back then and didn't get involved in such vices as crap games) would have felt the heavy hand of a policeman or prison "driver" with the cat-o-nine tails zipping all over his backside. In spite of threat of serious and immediate punishment for playing bonedice, some men still took chances. They gambled in secret places like in an abandoned house, in the sugarcane field, and even in the bull pen. But others were more bold. They rattled their dice in the open, under a taman tree, on the balcony of the "Children Home" in the evenings or on weekends when it was closed. By far, the most favorite place for gamblers was under the taman tree.

One evening, after they had retired from a grueling day in the canefield, a group of men came together under a taman tree to let off steam and roll bonedice. But someone had "an ax to grind" and called the police. When the policeman arrived, he parked his vehicle a good distance from where they were throwing dice and plenty bad-word. "See it yah. Tek it in yoh rass...WHAM! Ah comin' ahgain, WHAM...in yoh bottom...." He tried to step light, but the look-out man caught sight of him and gave the alarm. "POLICE! POLICE! Policeman ah come...." And the men ran like a bunch of frightened mongoose in all directions as the policeman opened fire. Bullets, real live bullets, tore through the dark night. Some ran into a canefield, others headed for the bush. But one man, Joe Ganz, sought refuge in a hog pen. As he jumped into the pen, a hog went "GRUFF, GRUFF." "SHIT, SHIT," said the man. "Ah me Joe Ganz ah run from bullet."

It was campaign time again, using the old politician style of coming face to face with small groups of people gathered in a yard or under a taman tree. This day a would-be councilman was trying his best to sell himself to the people. "My mother fought with me," he said. "She is the one.... She helped to make me the man that I am today." After the speech an old woman could hardly wait to speak her mind. Turning to a friend, she said "Sissi gel...sissi gel, meh noh ah goh vote foh Percy 'tall. 'Cause if he kin fight he mama, wen he geh een he sah kill ahwe."

Back in the old days, voting took place in Christiansted and Frederiksted. It was customary for candidates running for a seat in the Municipal Council to provide transportation for those people in the country who they believed would vote for them. One November a candidate who had sent his bus into the country to bring people to the polls lost the election and the poor country folks had to walk home. But one man even went a little further. When he learned that he was defeated, he approached the people seated in his bus waiting to be taken home. "Ah yoh...Ahyoh!" he shouted. "All ahyoh.... Tek ahyoh ma-ma rass out!.... All ahyoh ma-ma rass come out ah meh bus!"

Espousing the virtues of his good friend and humanitarian, Casper Holstein, before a large gathering, a man said, "Mr. Holstein...Mr. Holstein fart foh all ahyoh. An' if he been alive today he woulda been fartin' til now."

A politician came before the people one evening in Frederiksted under Free Gut taman tree. He was prepared to do battle in the upcoming election and was there to plead for votes. But there were a number of detractors in the crowd and they were ready for him. They were ready to "chook" him to the bone. "Ladies and gentleman," he said. "Ladies and gentlemen...." But he couldn't seem to get beyond those words. His detractors were taunting him without mercy. "Boo...boo...boo...boo .... Ahwe noh wan' yoh. Bu' look 'pon he. He wan' foh goh ah council, foh represent who? Not he mehson...." "Ladies and gentlemen," he continued amid the heckling, his face getting redder by the second. "Ladies and gentlemen...ladies and gentlemen," he said. "Ahyoh kiss meh rass. Goodnight!"

In the mid sixties, members of the Virgin Islands Democratic Party were battling one another. There were two factions: the Unity Party and the Donkey Democrats. The late Ralph Paiewonsky, Governor of the Virgin Islands, and Ron de

107

Lugo were on opposing sides. Aureo Diaz, who was running for office, supported Paiewonsky. In the heat of the battle, among other things Paiewonsky had called Ron de Lugo a "Juvenile Delinquent." Aureo Diaz took up the charge and now had his political sword "chooking" Ron's gullypipe (windpipe). As he mounted the rostrum one night, Diaz did not waste any time. Like a gamecock ready for blood, in two two's he had his spur in Ron de Lugo's behind. "De...De....De...." he said. "De...De...Ron de...de Lugo. He full ah...He...He full ah...He full ah...." "Shit!," yelled someone in the audience. "Yes, yes," said Diaz. "He full ah shit."

Ivan McIntosh, better known as Ivan "Wolf" or "'Tamper," was a musician who played the guitar and saxophone. I am not sure how he got the nickname Wolf, but the name 'Tamper stemmed from his musical experience. As the lead player in his band, he would stamp his big heavy foot three times on the dancehall floor to start the music. The crushing sound of Ivan "Wolf's" foot remained in the memory of his dancers and the nickname 'Tamper was born.

Ivan "Wolf" was also a man who owned and operated a taxi. His runs took him from Frederiksted to Christiansted and across the country. One day while driving on Centerline Road, he saw a woman standing on the side of the road. He stopped his taxi and said, "Yoh gwine up?" "Noh," said the woman. "Meh ah wait 'pon Ellick." Another day while on the same route, he spotted the woman and again he stopped his vehicle and said to the woman, "Yoh gwine up?" "Noh," replied the woman. "Meh ah wait 'pon Ellick." Ellick (Allick) Simmonds was a bus driver who went from Frederiksted to Christiansted about twice a day. A few days after, he came upon the same woman standing in the same spot on the road. This time it was pouring rain. Ivan "Wolf" quickly pulled his car next to her and said, "Miss, yoh gwine up?" "Yes," she said. "Ah gwine up." "'tand deh, wait 'pon Ellick," he said, and sped off into the rain.

The election fever was on. A politician was tearing his opponent to ribbons. Lashing out against his competitor for a seat in the Legislature, he said to his audience: "People! People! People! Let me tell you.... That man is a total scamp, ah lowdown no-good-dirty-dealing fellow. He is a sheep in Wolf's clothing. You heard what I said? Ladies and gentlemen, I repeat, he is a sheep in Wolf's clothing...." 'Tis then de joke tek.

Joseph Padmore (Paddy Moore)
Courtesy of Alda Forte.

PADDY DON'T DO IT

The name "Paddy Moore" has a ring to it. It is soft, and yet it rings loud. Mention the name to anyone who was born in West End or lived there in the twenties, thirties, and forties, or even before, and right away images of Joseph Padmore (Paddy Moore) flash across the screens of their minds: Creating, dancing, masquerading, blowing the tailpipe, playing drums, and more.

However, Emile Heywood, a native of West End, who was born in 1938, sees Paddy Moore in a different light. In his words:

> One pound of white flour mek two dumplin' foh Paddy. Dat's it, pot done! I have seen some strong men on dis island an' Paddy was top on de list. I knew Paddy Moore cuttin' wood an' burnin' coal. I knew him makin' brooms like those use' toh sweep de streets. I knew Paddy Moore wid a two-wheel cart. An' he pushed dat cart, fill wid coal an' brooms, from Frederiksted toh Christiansted, sold dem an' push de cart back toh Frederiksted. An' back den de roads were not as good as they are today. They were quite rough, gravel an' potholes. Yoh talk about strong? He was a beast!

> Paddy never drank a cold beer in his life. If yoh gave him six beers, he would leave dem 'til they got hot an' den drink dem. Da Paddy Moore deh.... A master man, S-T-R-O-N-G! He was an' ox, mehson.

Alexander Petersen, another native of West End, who was born in the late twenties and grew up in North Side, remembers

Alexander Petersen

Paddy Moore from the time he was a boy living at Estate Prosperity where Paddy also lived. Petersen tells a story about his old neighbor.

His real name was Joseph Padmore. There were two other siblings: Mrs. Susanna Padmore-Brathwaite and Alphonso Padmore. Paddy was born on St. Croix but lived in Santo Domingo. He was an actor and cultural bearer, a very creative man, and Crucian to his heart. Masquerading was his pleasure. Paddy made and wore attractive costumes. And he made them from just about anything he could get his hands on: banana leaves, bullrush (a plant which grows near water), canvas cloth, goat and sheep skin. He used glass, metal, and wood, to create a particular effect. For example, the pieces of glass sewn to his attire reflected the sun rays as he danced about. He was seldom without a mask and, as the artist he was, he used paint to its full advantage. And he was never without leggings which were made from women's old stockings. These ran from his knees and went over his bare feet to his instep.

But Paddy did more than make costumes and dance masquerade. He taught us his art. He showed us how to make drums—the kettle drum, snare drum, and bass drum. He taught us how to play the steel and blow the pipe. You call it "tailpipe." We called it the "ass pipe." He showed us how to blow it and suck up the air causing it to give a particular sound: BO-OP, BO-OP, BO-OP. All these things he taught us. We were little and didn't have the power in our lungs. But we practiced and practiced, and before long we had learned how to pump mouths full of air into the pipe to effect the desired sound. And I can't forget the tambourine and squash, all the instruments of a

Paddy Moore's "Tail Pipe" (the bass).

quelbe band. Paddy taught us, everyone.

Back to masquerading. Whenever Paddy performed he gave it all he had. It was masquerading time once more on July 4, 1933, and Paddy was dressed to kill: painted mask, bullrush skirt, and leggings. He was dancing his way through Frederiksted. As usual, he was a hit and the crowd followed and cheered him on: "Paddy, don' do it!" And he responded, "Yeh, ah gon doh it." And as they shouted, he danced for the better. He was prancing up and down and even began dancing on the ground. It was then that someone threw a lighted cigarette on him and all of a sudden there was a puff of smoke. The people—who thought that it was another of Paddy's acts—did nothing to put out the fire, but waited in eager anticipattion for his next act. But when the smoke turned to flames and Paddy got up and started running down the street, they ran behind him. He dashed down Queen Cross Street and right into the sea. It was a cruel, crazy game to play on anyone. Paddy spent a few days in the hospital and was soon released. However, the incident did not dampen his masquerading spirit. He kept on!

According to one source, the man who threw the lighted cigarette on Paddy, said that Paddy was "plehin' de devil. An' if de devil deh ah hell he must gah fire 'round he rass."

Paddy was an epileptic. We saw him suffer several seizures. Once while cooking he fell over the pot and one hand dropped into the boiling pot of rice and peas, remaining there for a little while before someone realized what had happened and quickly came to his aid. Again Paddy spent some time in the hospital, but before long he was out and back on his feet dancing.

Paddy loved dancing, dancing was his t'ing. He had more nish (style) as they say "than John read 'bout." And he was indeed a very creative dancer. But he often got in a frenzy, got completely carried away. And what might have been a very good performance one minute, in the eyes of some turned tasteless, especially when children were around—and they were often present when Paddy went beyond his normal routine. One day the music was blazing and Paddy got so worked up he went beyond normal limits. He went wild, shaking his frame and "wukkin up," causing a woman to shout, "Paddy, don't do it! Don't do it, Paddy." And he responded, "Yeh, ah gon do it," and he danced for the better. And the woman kept up: "Paddy, ah seh don' do it." And he continued, "Yeh, ah gon do it...." "Don't do it" soon became Paddy's nickname and all one had to do to get him carried away while dancing was to say, "Paddy, don't do it. Don't do it, Paddy" and he would go off.

Paddy was a great masquerader and dancer who, among other things, made his living as a sugarcane field worker. But even though he would put in long hard hours in the sugarcane fields, when he got home in the afternoon he was never too tired to turn to his creative ventures such as making a drum or other items. And whenever Paddy made something, he started from scratch. For example, when making a drum he would kill a goat and place the skin in the sun to dry until it became very hard. He would then cover the hair with sand, take a gadget with a beveled edge (which he had made himself), and rub the sand over the skin, removing all of the hair. He would rub it until was completely white. Next he wetted the skin, making it supple to fit over the keg which he had already made.

Paddy was also a utility man. He taught us how to make ropes. He took caretta, pound it, and scraped off the green pulp, placing the threads in the sun to dry. They were then plaited into strong ropes which he sold to fishermen, farmers, and others. Sometimes it was hard to tell the difference between ropes in the stores and the ones Paddy made. He was very good at it. And he was very good at stilling booze too, out there in Prosperity bush. I learned to still booze from Paddy and my grandfather (who was from Barbados and lived in the rain forest). I didn't know anything about Prohibition then. It was some time after I became a student that I learned about the Eighteenth Amemdment to the United States Constitution. One day I was out there in the rain forest with my grandfather when policeman Charles Patrick rode up on his horse. It was Prohibition time but I didn't know it. My grandfather used to make his booze and I used to hide it in the ground under the silk cotton tree. I knew how to protect my grandfather's supply. Policeman Patrick and my grandfather were quite social—I had seen them chatting before. That day when he was about to leave, he said to my grandfather, "Well, it would be nice if I could get a cool one to hit the road." "Sorry," my grandfather replied, "ah can't help yoh wid dat 'cause ah ain' gah noh booze." I thought for a moment, then I said "Bu' grandfather, we gah ah drink o' booze we could gi'e he." And he said, "Well, yoh seh e gah booze. Yoh gi'e he." And so I went, got the booze and gave policeman Patrick some in a little cup. And he said, "Man! This is good stuff." After he drank the booze, he and my grand- father continued to chat for a little while. Then he said: "Look, deh send me out here toh look foh booze. Bu' ah ain' see noh booze yet. Bu' jus' talk toh de li'l fella deh. He

117

mean well, bu' he coulda geh yoh in trouble, if it was somebody else." Well, let me tell you, that's the only whipping I ever got from my grandfather. After that day, I never talk out of turn.

Back to Paddy Moore: masquerader, dancer, craftsman, and cultural bearer. Very few could match his performance. He had Crucian culture deeply rooted in him and he passed it on.

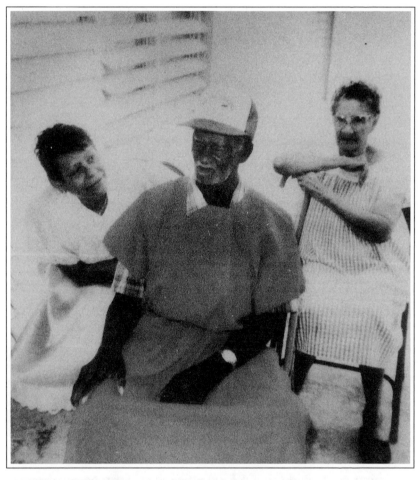

1984 Whim Gardens home for aged. Paddy Moore in his masquerade dress ready to perform, but changed his mind when he learned that there would be no live music. Nurse Susana Rivera and Fransica Sicar looks on.
Courtesy: Luz Minerva Nazario and Noemi Osorio.

"FRANKIE PETE" OF WEST END

Few people on St. Croix can say that they have lived on this island, in the same house for seventy years and more. But Frankie Pete (Frank Petersen) can. He has lived at 43 Queen Street, Frederiksted, in the same house where he was born to Hugh and Petrina Petersen seventy years ago. Frankie, who was educated in the town of his birth, was taught by Otis Brown, Claude O. Markoe and Alexander Moorhead. "Otis Brown never used to play," said Frankie. "He whipped between ten to twenty children in a single day. He would line them up until he was ready. Then took them one by one in the "operation room" where he administered the leatherstrap across their backs. And don't curse or say any bad word and let him hear you. He had a remedy for that. The punishment was one spoon of castor oil. No 'ifs' nor 'buts.' You had to take it. 'Come here sonny. You have a nasty mouth. Here is a little castor oil to clean you out.'"

According to Frankie Pete, Claude O. Markoe was a very good math teacher. Many years later that same math taught by Mr. Markoe helped him through same rough spots at Rochester University. Alexander Moorhead, who was educated at Hampton Institute, Virginia, was his history teacher. And although it has been nearly sixty years since Frankie sat in his classroom, he remembers one of Moorhead's examination questions: 'What effect did the fall of the Roman Empire had on modern society?' "I believe he brought that one from Hampton," said Frankie. He was not a teacher who gave easy test questions like True and False. And when he gave an examination, he didn't remain in the classroom to see who was going to cheat. You had to study for his examinations. No beating around the bush. You either knew the answer or you didn't.

119

Frank Petersen (Frankie Pete).

Some children were always making pranks at school. Walter I.M. Hodge (Brother Hodge) was the chief prankster. One day he threw a bucket of water on a teacher who was smoking in the toilet, then ran to the principal's office and yell: 'Fire! Fire! Mr. Markoe...Mr. Markoe, de toilet deh on fire!' Brother Hodge, the practical joker, was always scheming for ways to make us laugh. Phillip Rosenthal, a Danish boy, was a classmate. One day Brother Hodge said to him, "Phillip, yoh want toh buss some fart in school?" "Yes, said Phillip with a big grin. "OK," said Brother Hodge. "Ah gon bring something foh yoh tomorrow." The next day he brought sulphur to school and gave it to Phillip who swallowed it. Before long he had light-up the whole classroom. All you could hear was: Boop. Boop. Boop.... "Oh!" said Mr. Markoe. "Phillip...Phillip, you're not feeling well today." And as he said 'today,' the bombs began to fall again. Boop. Boop. Boop.... It was so bad, Phillip had to go home.

Many young men left the island in the early forties to enter military service. But Frankie enlisted in another service, he remained on the homefront caring for the sick. He joined the staff at Frederiksted Municipal Hospital, fresh out of high school. And for the next thirty-eight years worked in every division in health care in the Virgin Islands Health Service, retiring in 1979 as supervisor of X-ray Services. However, Frankie's concern was not just limited to health care. The social and political needs of St. Croix constantly tugged at his heart: terrible housing conditions, the nightsoil system, high infant mortality, and the policital clubs which catered to the needs of a few.

In 1951, Frankie returned home after a course of study on health issues at the University of Rochester, New York. His exposure abroad helped him to focus anew on the problems at home.

Around the same time many of the men who had gone off to the military service during World War II were also returning. They saw the conditions, and given their experiences and exposure in the United States, they too wanted to do something about it. The first order of business was to change the "Old Guard." But that was no easy task. In those days Virgin Islands politics was controled by the property class or the "Well-toh-doh." It was the time of political clubs, which called the shots and decided who would run for office and who would not. It was a clique. And as the old people say, "If you didn't belong 'toh the clique dawg better than yoh.'" "They were closed shops," said Frankie. "And if you didnt have some money in the bank, land or other property, the people who ran the clubs tended to look down on you. I remember the day in 1947 when I registered to vote for the first time. It was a grand day of my life. I felt so proud, very good about myself. But I could sense the feeling of those present. The look on their faces said it all. 'Here comes big mouth. Why is this young boy want to get in this t'ing for? Who does he think he is? This is our t'ing. We run it.'"

Back to the fifties. So here we were, a group of men and women on St. Croix and another group on St. Thomas led by Earl B. Ottley, who wanted piece of the Virgin Islands political pie and planning ways to get some. There was no Democratic Primary election. While travelling in the United States, when I told a fellow Democrat that one of the things we were fighting for in the Virgin Islands was the right to conduct primary elections, he laughed. "You don't have to fight for that," he said. "It is all part of the political system of the United States. The people choose who they want to represent them, not the political bosses."

The matter came to a head in the early sixties, when

122

the Old Guard, the Donkey Democrats took us, the Unity Party, 'Mortar and Pestle' to court, saying that were trying to take over the Democratic Party in the Virgin Islands. They lost and we won the right to have Democratic Primary elections.

New blood was infused into the political system, with such candidates for senatorial office as: Patrick "Pat" Williams, Dr. Randall "Doc" James, and several others on St. Croix and St. Thomas. Little by little things began to improve. The housing situation got better. The nightsoil system came to an end in Christiansted and Frederiksted. There was more running water in homes. And overall, health conditions were on the upswing.

Frankie Pete was the first State Chairman for the Democratic Party in the Virgin Islands. He never held a seat in the senate, but has received international recognition for his work with the JC's (Junior Chamber of Commerce) as 'senator for life.'

In 1980 the Legislature of the U.S. Virgin Islands passed Resolution No. 996, Bill No. 13-0415 honoring Frankie Pete for his many years of service in the health care of the Virgin Islands: a registered nurse, laboratory technologist, environmental sanitarian and specialist in radiological technology. Among other accomplishments, Frankie also helped to organize the first blood bank on St. Croix.

But that's only one side of him. Frankie Pete is a real Crucian—as Crucian as boil fish and okra fungi. He is a man with a bag of stories and a belly full of laughs. Here is the other side of Frankie.

Frankie, tell me about the old days in Frederiksted when you were a boy.

123

Let's start with masquerading. Unlike today, the groups were not all that organized. There was no Festival Committee. People did very much their own thing. Some groups came from the country. One group would go down one street and a second group another. The performers, who wore masks and other costumes, would sing and dance quelbe as they moved through the town. Some would stop at our house and my parents would offer them drinks, guavaberry rum, a few pennies, or whatever they had. All groups would convene at one point and have one big showdown, a real blowout, everybody singing, dancing, and jumping up. At the end of the day, those people from the country walked back to their villages and that was the end of it, until the next holiday. However, before the masquerading began around midday, there were small groups that came out very early in the morning around 5:00 a.m., playing music on the tailpipe, steel, squash, banjo, and other instruments. They went from house to house in great merriment, singing, making little speeches to get you in the Christmas spirit. And, of course, the folks would respond with food, drink, and a little money.

We're talking about the thirties and forties?

Yes. Now at Easter time there was also another celebration. That's the time when the David and Goliath groups were in swing, men decked out in such costumes as goatskins and sheepskins, carrying bamboo staffs and wooden swords. And little David was among them with his slingshot. The play was performed in the streets. A man by the name of Marshall, who was also a moko jumbie dancer and fisherman (who mainly caught lobsters) was one of the leading players.

124

Getting back to Christmas, there was this man, his name was Cornell. He was very dark, a tall man who wore an earring in his right or left ear. He lived at Wheel of Fortune (Harden). Every Christmas he came to town playing a tambourine. Man, I tell you, he really played that thing, going from steeet to street. But even though he lived just about a mile from Frederiksted, that was the only time he came to town. He was a one-man band. And he sang and "throwdown" music, music ringing in the air.

There was a man at Fredensborg where I grew up. His name was Arthur Weeks. He was a master on the tambourine. He could make it talk. When he scraped his thumb on that tambourine, you felt it in your bones. I have never met anyone who could play that instrument like him. He died playing his tambourine.

Christimas was really a time of coming together in song, dance, and music. that was mainly my experience about it.

Now a little about the food we ate. Speaking from personal experience, chicken was not an everyday dish. It was a big treat at Christmas. We would kill about three to four chickens and make chicken soup or chicken and rice. We also had stuffing and other trimmings. Most people raised chickens but mainly for the eggs. They were raised in a limited quantity. You couldn't kill your chickens and have your eggs too. We used eggs in cakes and ice cream. Occasionally we would have eggs for breakfast. Very seldom you would find people cooking chicken on a regular basis like today. Chicken was mainly a holiday meal. The main staples were pork, goat, and fish. My mother never ate any food or cooked anything that was more than a few hours old. When she ate goat or pork, she got it from the man just down the street, who brought it to our house. We were usually his first customers. Nothing was stale; everything was butchered and cooked on the same day. Although there was a fish market in those days, we didn't go to the fish market. The fisherman brought fish to our house. He came about 9:00 a.m. and we selected what fish we wanted. The same with vegetables. There was the vegetable market a few blocks away, but our vegetables were brought directly to us by people from North Side. I suppose that's why my mother lived to the ripe old age of 95. She ate everything fresh. It is true that we might not have had a balanced diet as we have today, but the food was fresh.

Let's turn to Paddy Moore and some of the other characters of your time. How long have you known Paddy Moore?

I had known Paddy from the time I was a boy about ten years old. Later on I learned that he was the last person to wear African costumes during the holidays while masquerading. He was usually dressed in an outfit made from bullrush or banana leaves. I understand that they used the same costumes in West Africa during ceremonial affairs.

While masquerading, Paddy would be dancing up a breeze amid a shower of music from the flute, goatskin drum, steel, squash, and tailpipe. Sometimes Paddy played the goatskin drum. He also enjoyed blowing the tailpipe, on which he was a master. One day while dancing in the street, dressed down in his bullrush/banana leaves costume, a man lit a match and set him on fire. He ran to the sea near the old ice factory on Strand Street and threw himself in the water. Luckily the burns were not severe.

It was said that Paddy was sent to prison here in Frederiksted for an offense he had committed. Paddy was a dumplin' man, he loved his dumplin', bull tongue dumplin'. But the dumplings they served one day at prison were not to Paddy's liking and he complained about it. He said a dumplin' must be thick, thick—when you put your teeth in it, it must say "click." If it doesn't say "click," it is not a proper dumplin', it wasn't kneaded well. And Paddy loved his cornpork too. I have never seen him eating any vegetables like tomatoes, lettuce, carrots, and the like. But I believe he supplemented his diet with fruits. He was a hard-working man, strong as an ox.

Years ago people went to the gut for gravel to build houses. One day Paddy was given a job to load a truck with gravel in the La Vallee area. He completed the job. But when the driver tried to get the truck going, he couldn't. The heavy load was too much, resulting in broken springs and damage to the transmission. Paddy then walked from La Vallee to Frederiksted and went around town saying how he had "bruckdown a truck in La Vallee gut wid wuk." "Ah bruk um down toh de ground—meh, Paddy, doh um," he said, slapping his chest. "Meh noh ah pleh. Bruk um right down, ah seh out deh ina La Vallee gut."

Late one evening Paddy was on his way home from Christiansted to Frederiksted. He went through Grove Place. As he walked by, he heard the sound of music coming from one of the nightspots. A quelbe band was playing. Everything seemed alright except for the man blowing the tailpipe. "Noh sah," said Paddy. "Da t'ing ain' sound right. Ah gon' help out ahyoh." And he went all the way to Frederiksted, got his own tailpipe, went back to Grove, and played all night.

And speaking of the tailpipe (which was really an exhaust pipe from a car), it couldn't be used just like that. It had to be properly cleaned, treated, and cured. You put hot sand in it and bent it into shape, so that sound may flow. Next you poured sweet oil in it and let it set awhile. Only then it was ready for the pipeman's lips.

Paddy was a master masquerader and pipeman. He lived for many years in Santo Domingo and spoke fluent Spanish. He was over 90 years old when he died in February 1995.

There was another man—I don't remember his name. However, he was a great performer and was called "Suzzy and Mikey" after the act he performed. Several of his toes were missing, but that didn't seem to bother him. He sat with strings tied around his big toes, with two little dolls, "Suzzy and Mikey," extended from the strings. He played his guitar, twiddled his toes, and the dolls danced from opposite ends of the string and met at the center. It was a real art form. Whenever Suzzy and Mikey sat down to play his guitar, those dolls dancing on a string, a crowd always gathered, and pennies, nickels, and dimes were thrown into a hat near him. In spite of his deformity, he was such a happy person, always in a jovial mood with a good joke to tell.

What about Mr. Halliday? Do you recall him?

Sure. He was another great performer. His name was

Albert Halliday. He loved to sing, dance, and tell stories. One of his favorite pieces was "Tanto Li-za." He also liked to pretend he was reading from a book, a ledger or Sears Roebuck catalog. As the calypsonians did with their songs, he too did with his make-up speeches. He didn't call any names. But everyone knew who he was talking about. He told humorous tales about politicians and other government officials. Some people were afraid of him because if they did anything out-the-way, when the holidays came around Albert Halliday would make a speech about it and everyone would know.

Any more stories?

A lady who lived down the street from us had a number of crabs in a barrel. She was preparing them for the kallaloo she had planned to cook. She had purged the crabs with cornmeal. But the crabs were always crawling over each other in the barrel, trying to get to the top and get out before the lady placed a pot of hot water on the fire. Consequently, there were always dead crabs in the barrel, which the lady removed daily. There was a man who did some work around the house. One morning, just as the lady was taking the dead crabs out of the barrel, he walked in the yard. "Miss," he said, "what are you doing?" "I am throwing away these dead crabs," she answered. "Noh! Noh! Noh, Missis," said the man. "Dem kin boil! Dem kin boil!" He didn't know it then but he had earned a nickname that would last a lifetime: "Dem kin boil."

Let's talk about the old policemen of Frederiksted. Anyone in particular comes to mind?

Yes. Eugene Bennerson. He was a nice man but a no-nonsense policeman who liked to butt. If you were out of order and he had to arrest you, he might quicker use head on you than his club. During World War II, we had the 806 Engineers stationed here. When they came to town, some of them could get very nasty after they had a couple drinks. One day this huge soldier was really playing de ass. He had a lot of rum in his head and it was controlling him. It looked as though he couldn't wait to go to war. Everyone around seemed to be the enemy. Bennerson, who was on patrol, warned him to stop the nonsense. And the soldier turned on him, cursing him and using racial remarks. And Bennerson put down his club, grabbed him, and buss him one butt. The soldier reeled like a cock hit with a bad spur and fell to the ground.

I knew a man who delivered a crush butt to his donkey's head when the animal refused to pull the cart. When the donkey received the blow he was away. Also, if someone was running away from a policeman, I heard that some of the police were good at throwing a club between the person's legs, causing him to trip and fall.

I don't know about that but I know about *stickfighting*—I have seen it.

Tell me about it.

There was this fellow. His name was Thadeus but he was called "Lion." Lion was a famous stickfighter. He was good. When I say good, I mean good. That man could knock out your toenail without touching your foot. He was one of the best stickfighters around.

How was stickfighting conducted? Was it a sport, like boxing or wrestling?

130

I believe that stickfighting came to us from Africa. It is also found in Robin Hood stories. Some way along the line, I believe it was adopted and became part of our culture.

Was there a prize given to the winner of a stickfighting match?

Most of the stickfights which took place, as I remember, resulted from some disagreement, with one man challenging another. Or in the case of self defense. A story goes that one night a man who considered himself as a "bad man" was at a dance. He had had a few drinks and spat on the ground. Then gave a challenge. He said, "If anyone in here think he badder than me, let him spit on my spit." As the words dropped, a topnotch stickfighter stepped from out the crowd with a stick in his hand. When the supposedly "bad man" saw him, he got sober right away. "Oh God!" he said. "Man...man.... Ah ain' know yoh been yah. Ah gone. See ahyoh, yoh hear."

Any stories about the old fishermen?

Although there were fishermen with many years of experience at sea in small rowboats or sailboats, not all of them could swim. Brother Licrish, a very religious man, was such a person. He couldn't swim an inch. And yet he was out in the sea nearly five days a week. He fell overboard several times and had to be rescued. But that did not stop him going to fish. And to compound the problem, no one used a life jacket in those days. But, as the saying goes, God never takes you before your time. Brother Licrish died peacefully in his bed one day.

Who was "King" Barnes?

"King" Barnes was another character. He always carried a big crocus bag over his shoulder. And in that bag were yams, potatoes, limes, lemons, avocados, or whatever were in season. Yet he had no land. He was giving those Northside farmers a run for their fruits and provisions. They tried to catch him but never could. They swore, however, that if they ever caught him stealing their goods, they would surely "cook e sauce." One man made a boast. He said King Barnes could never steal anything from his land and get away with it. He said he had his place "fix," that even if King Barnes got in, he couldn't get out before he comes. Even if it took two days for him to arrive. King Barnes had no choice. He had to stand right there. He couldn't leave. The man was dealing in obeah. He said he had found a good jumbie to put on King Barnes to make him stop his stealing. When King Barnes heard what the man had said, he said "Cha! He can't doh meh ah damn t'ing. Ah can goh anywhere ah want toh." And so one day he went in the man's land and picked two bags of mangoes. But when he started to leave, he heard a voice say, "Whe yoh gwine!" It was the jumbie the man had gotten to stop King Barnes. He ain' say a word but quickly turned around and began walking backwards until he was out of the man's land. He had confused the jumbie who had expected to come forward. When the people saw King Barnes selling mangoes in town, they were quite surprised. They had thought King Barnes had met his match. But not so. He had outsmarted the same jumbie the man had put in his land to stop him.

But King Barnes was the exception rather than the rule?

Oh, yes. Most people didn't do that sort of thing.

When I was a boy, people generally didn't go around taking things that did not belong to them. I would often hear the words "Mehson, meh noh ah tief. Meh wuk hard foh wha meh gah." What are your thoughts about the old Frederiksted as compared with the Frederiksted of today?

In many respects we are living better than we ever did before. Medical care has improved. We have moved from the donkey cart to the car; from the coalpot to the stove; from the goose to the electric iron; and from the washtub to the washing machine. No doubt we have and are enjoying a host of conveniences. In many ways modern-day living is great. But it was something about life in the old days. . . . First of all, let's take crime. I remember the days when murder was a very rare occurrence on St. Croix. And when a murder did occur, everywhere you turned people would be talking about it. And they would talk about it for a year or more. Today people killing people like they would kill goat. Murder is too common an occurrence. In the old days there was greater respect for life and the law as a whole. Back then, a teacher was like a parent, they had authority. If a teacher met you on the street doing something you shouldn't be doing and that teacher said "go home," you went home. And other older persons in the community had the same authority to correct wrong behavior on the spot. Sometimes you didn't even have to be doing something wrong for a teacher or other older person to intervene. "Schoolboy, yoh deh on de street toh long; ah sure yoh mother lookin' foh yoh. Goh home!" And you went home. Because if the teacher or older person met your mother the next day and told her that he or she spoke to you, you were in a lot of trouble. There was a lot of respect for authority and the law which is practically gone today. That is not to say that the people were angels in those days. There were the characters who drank too much, or one man might knife another in a gambling house. But generally people were more respectful. There was more tranquility. And another thing, people would help each other. I remember when my mother was a godmother to half a dozen children and helped raise those same children in addition to her own. Those were some of the good things, not only about old Frederiksted, but old St. Croix as a whole.

GLOSSARY

Ah	a, an, at, I, is, of
Ahright	OK, alright
Ahwe	us, all of us
Ahyoh	all of you
Ba ba	baby
Bass	boss
Bateau	flat-bottomed boat
Beel	car
Booku	loads of, plenty
Bottom foot	under surface of the foot
Bu'	but
Buckra	white man
Buss	burst
Canepiece	sugarcane field
Caretta	a plant whose fiber is used to make mats, ropes, and other ornaments
Carousel	merry-go-round
Cata (kata)	rolled-cloth or leaves used as a cushion on the head for carrying a heavy basket, bucket of water, tray with food or other goods
Children Home	nursery school on sugarcane estate
Chook	to stick or prick, to put, to play a game as in "Chook Cusho" (cashew), to jab or prod

Cocobay	leprosy
Cook e sauce	to get even
Coolie	an East Indian, unskilled laborer
Cooping	to follow another's action shyly
Crocus bag	burlap sack
Dah (Dat, Da)	that
Dane School	Public Elementary School built by the Danes
De	the
Deh	they, their, there
Dem	them
Den	then
Dis	this
Doan	don't
Doh	do
Dum-johnny cake	Unleavened baked-johnny cake
E	it, he, she, his, her, him
Eba	ever
Ebry	every
Een	in
Fraico	ice cone
Foh	for
Fungi (Fungee)	boiled cornmeal dish

Gah	has, have
Galvanize	iron sheet coated with zinc to prevent rust, house covering
Gawn	go, go ahead
Geh	get
Gel	girl
Gon	going, gone, went
Gri Gri	a tree once used to make shafts for ox, horse and mule carts
Gwine	going to
Haus	horse
Hoosha	wheel of varied sizes with guide made from palm tree, wood or wire
Ina (Inna)	in, into
Kafoon	to fall headlong, somersault
Kin	can
Larrum	disturbance, trouble
Lawd	Lord
Leba	liver
Leh	let
Licking	beating
Lil	little, small
Lodgin'	bedding, clothing
Manjah	manager

Marnin	morning
Meh	me, mine, my
Mehson	my son
Mek	make, made
Melee	story, gossip
Mocolabe	utterly foolish person
Mo'	more, must
Mudda	mother
Ninyam	food
Nish	style
Noh	no
Nuff	enough, ample
Nuttin	nothing
Outa	out of
Peh Peh	Godfather
Pleh	play
Pon	on, upon
Pon-ta-pah	on top of
Ra-Ra	a toy
Runwey	run away
Sah	sir, will do
Seh	say, said

Soh	so
Shub	to force
Santapee	centipede
Taman (Tambrand)	tamarind
Tan Tan	name of a tree, aunt
Tania	vegetable cooked and eaten like yam or potato
Tipet	Thibet tree
Toh	to, too
T'reefoot	steel implement with three legs (a pot is placed on a t'ree foot over fire for cooking)
Um	it
Under de Taman Tree	under the Tamarind Tree
Wha	what
Wid	with
Whe	where
Wrang	wrong
Wuk	work
Wus	was
Yah	here
Yeh	yes
Yoh	you

ABOUT THE AUTHOR

RICHARD A. SCHRADER, a retired prison warden and soldier turned writer, first took up the pen in 1984 to write poetry on Blue Mountain, St. Croix, Virgin Islands, and has not put it down since.

In addition to writing eight books, he has contributed to "Collage One, Two and Three" and several other publications.

He is the recipient of the Virgin Islands Housing Authority Cultural Preservation Award, Rotary International Paul Harris Fellowship Award, and was The Virgin Islands Humanities Council 1994 "Humanist of the Year," in recognition of his tireless efforts in preserving the traditional culture of St. Croix.

Schrader and his wife, Claudette, reside at Calquohoun, just a short distance from the old village where he was born.